Garibaldi Provincial Park, British Columbia

Waking Up the West Coast
Healers and Visionaries

Photographed and edited by Jaime Kowal
Foreword by Dr Andrew Weil

CATALYST
PUBLICATIONS

First edition

Text © Catalyst Publications 2006
Photos © Jaime Kowal Photography 2006

Published by Catalyst Publications
www.catalystpublications.com
info@catalystpublications.com

For orders and customer service, call 1.866.840.1711. Distributed to the book trade by New Society Publishers—Books that provide positive solutions for troubled times. For book trade orders, call 1.800.567.6772

Book design by Cardeo Creative
www.cardeo.ca

Additional design by Cowie and Fox Creative

Printed and bound in Canada by Hemlock Printers

Library of Congress cataloguing-in-publication data: A catalogue record for this publication is available from the National Library of Canada.

ISBN-10: 0-9739088-0-7
ISBN-13: 978-0-9739088-0-0

Catalyst Publications is an ethical publishing company dedicated to promoting positive growth and connecting conscious consumers with socially responsible sustainable businesses, organizations and practitioners. Our books help you make informed decisions that promote personal and planetary health. They act as a catalyst, educating, inspiring and empowering you and your community to make positive, everyday choices that, collectively, have a big impact.

A percentage of the proceeds from this book are being donated to the Weil Foundation (www.weilfoundation.org) and the Health Action Network Society (www.hans.org).

This book has been made possible by the financial and other contributions made by the contributors herein. The claims made by each contributor featured in this publication are the claims of that particular contributor. Each contributor has been given the opportunity to personally edit their text. Reasonable and considerable effort has been made by the author and publisher to ensure accuracy; however, it is essential for readers to conduct their own analysis of the contributors' business activities prior to engaging their service(s).

The information in this book is accurate and complete, to the best of our knowledge. It is intended to provide snapshots of selected individuals actively engaged in their respective fields and to serve as a general guide to the industry categories featured. This publication should not be considered a source of medical information or an endorsement of any contributor contained herein. Readers should consult their healthcare practitioner before engaging in any alternative form of treatment. All recommendations are made without guarantee on the part of the authors or Catalyst Publications.

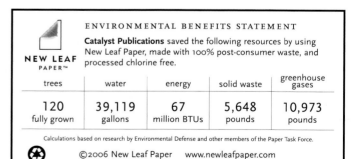

ENVIRONMENTAL BENEFITS STATEMENT

Catalyst Publications saved the following resources by using New Leaf Paper, made with 100% post-consumer waste, and processed chlorine free.

trees	water	energy	solid waste	greenhouse gases
120 fully grown	39,119 gallons	67 million BTUs	5,648 pounds	10,973 pounds

Calculations based on research by Environmental Defense and other members of the Paper Task Force.

©2006 New Leaf Paper   www.newleafpaper.com

"New Leaf Paper's mission is to lead the paper industry toward sustainability with our product line of cutting-edge environmentally responsible papers. New Leaf Paper is proud to supply the paper for this book, which is filled with people and stories that inspire us in our work."

-Jeff Mendelsohn, President

TABLE OF CONTENTS

ACKNOWLEDGEMENTS

I would like to thank the following:

Each and every contributor for their dedication, energy and belief in the vision of this project. This book would not exist without you!

Dr Andrew Weil for honouring all of the contributors and their hard work in his foreword to this book. Andrew has changed countless lives through his thorough, eloquent teachings and is a shining example of how one individual can have an enormous impact.

Vancity for their generous donation, which has allowed us the opportunity to make choices that support the highest environmental standards, including printing locally and employing 100% post-consumer-waste recycled New Leaf paper. We are excited to participate in Vancity's 'Granting for Carbon Offsets Pilot Project,' as part of their commendable goal of making their company carbon-neutral by 2010. Participating in this pilot project has allowed us to save the 135 tonnes of CO_2e (carbon dioxide equivalent) that would have been expended if we had printed the book offshore. This is the equivalent of taking 27 cars off the road for an entire year! I would like to thank Matt Tidwell from The Climate Trust for so readily calculating this profound projection for us, and Derek Gent from Vancity for recognizing this project's potential.

Renewal Partners for their amazing moral, logistical and financial support. The experience, perspective and dedication of Joel Solomon and his team have enabled us to take this project to a higher level, introducing us to key players in the exciting world of socially responsible business.

Aron Bjornson of Capers Community Markets for believing in our vision right from the start. Capers' inspiring commitment to continually support their local community in creative ways is to be commended, and has enabled us to feature a number of non-profit organizations in this book.

My mother, Susan Kowal, for her tireless efforts and dedication in managing the innumerable details involved in the production and management of this book; my writers, editors and copyeditors, especially Olga Sheean for her amazing devotion to the written word and for embracing this project heart and soul, as well as Chris Tyrell, Marilyn J. Milne, Karen Kwan, Sonja Rasula, Randi-

Lee Taylor, Sandra Ferens, Andre LaRiviere and Erica Gerhke, who handled the creative challenge of capturing the spirit of each contributor and channeling it into 300 words in such an elegant way; New Society Publishers for opening the doors of international distribution to the book trade; Matt Lambert of Cardeo Creative for his thorough attention to detail and for the clean, dynamic, aesthetic design; Cowie and Fox for the creative brainstorming and development of our look; Kim Zaragoza, Sanae Okada, Corsini Walker, Sarah Mushansky, Serena McKean, Tami Lim, Rachel Davis, Davis Webb, Laura Adrain, Brandy Laderoute, Dana Mooney, Nitasha Najeeb, Chelsi Middleton and Shareen Abdul-Mumin, my make-up artists who embarked with such joy and curiosity on this adventure; Laura Gray and Nicole Lino, my wardrobe stylists; Jacques Choquette for all the late nights spent developing and programming our fabulous, functional website; Sharon Richlark for her support, wisdom and guidance in keeping me healthy and energized throughout this marathon of a project; Bobbi Van Riet for helping to co-create the concept in such a fun way; Wayne Hoerchal for facilitating the colour corrections on the photos; Mark Leibowitz for capturing my energy and spirit in his photo of me on the introduction page; Deirdre Rowland of Cme Publicity for fully embracing the vision of this project and being so passionate about getting the word out on the street; Rebecca Ephraim and Ron Williams of Shared Vision for featuring excerpts of the book in their inspirational magazine and being so enthusiastic about the project in general; Mark Benda for educating me so thoroughly about Internet strategy and messaging; Jan Mills for her creative ideas and mentorship; Dustin Nestor for his clarity and logical accounting mind; Gordon McGarrigle for his patient business support; Christine Hwang for creating such a beautiful photographic backdrop; and, of course, my family and friends for their advice, perspective, constant encouragement and unconditional love—especially my parents, Don and Susan, and my sister Ainsley. I couldn't have done this without you!

FOREWORD

By Dr Andrew Weil

Waking Up the West Coast: Healers and Visionaries takes a unique approach to integrative living. It not only features individuals and organizations working in holistic and integrative medicine, but also promotes awareness of the importance of informed decision-making in *all* areas of life, providing opportunities for us all to engage in our community and support socially responsible businesses and investors, environmental activists, progressive educators, independent media, organic farmers and those working in health and wellness.

Like me, Jaime is dedicated to providing tools to help others integrate healthy choices into their lives. And just as integrative medicine strives to engage patients as active participants in their own healthcare through education, empowered decision-making and mind-body therapies, the wide array of contributors featured here promote self-responsibility and awareness across the entire spectrum of human activity—from personal healing to environmental stewardship.

Jaime is a gifted and talented photographer. Her ability to capture authentic expression and emotion in each photograph, combined with her dedication to educate and inspire, makes for an uplifting read. This book puts a personal face on today's hot issues, offering practical, tangible ways for you to become empowered and involved in your life and community. Dive in, enjoy the rich imagery, savour the inspiration, examine the ways you can integrate and utilize these resources in your life, and then act! Discuss these ideas with your family, friends and communities. Introduce this book to your reading circles. Try something new and observe how your life and the lives of those around you begin to evolve and improve. This book was designed as a catalyst for positive change; please use it to help create a healthier, more sustainable future for us all.

INTRODUCTION

By Jaime Kowal

This book introduces you to the vast wealth of passion, knowledge and experience that exists on Canada's West Coast, promoting optimal health, supportive relationships, informed consumer choices, a just society and a healthier planet. A hothouse of talent, British Columbia is well known for its strong economy, government initiatives, beautiful landscapes, political freedom, pioneering spirit and environmental leadership. These factors foster a strong sense of community and a commitment to ongoing sustainability and excellence.

A visually compelling showcase, this book profiles 118 BC-based socially-conscious businesses, non-profit organizations, holistic health practitioners, educators, artists and activists who exemplify leadership and creativity, and who are dedicated to helping educate and inspire individuals to conscious action. Their expertise runs the full gamut—from building eco-friendly communities, creating new technologies and promoting self-responsibility, to offering integrated health services and saving millions of acres of old-growth forest. Yet they have one thing in common: they are dedicated to making this world a better place by actively following their hearts and passions. No matter where you live, you can benefit from the innovative tools, creative ideas and smart solutions provided by this talented, dedicated group. I encourage you to follow their lead and incorporate even just one idea or suggestion and see how it enhances your life, family and/or community.

In today's media-driven society, we are constantly bombarded with depressing news about the state of our world—climate change, biodiversity loss, freshwater shortages, endless wars, skyrocketing disease—and we often end up focusing on what's not working instead of what is. This book offers you the opportunity to shift your perspective and realize that you can make positive, responsible choices that foster a more sustainable, harmonious, planet-friendly lifestyle. It can help you make decisions that count.

We, as consumers, have access to more information now than ever before. This means we can leverage our purchasing power to influence the way businesses operate and to promote greater accountability in the corporate world. We make a difference with each grocery purchase we make, every charity we support, and every new treatment we explore in the pursuit of better health.

These decisions can be fun, easy to implement and seemingly insignificant, yet collectively they make a big difference. When enough of us do the same thing, we reach what is known as the "tipping point"—the point at which our individual efforts reach critical mass, tipping the balance in our favour. Whether it's a technology, procedure, service or philosophy, it becomes part of the mainstream when the tipping point is reached.

This cumulative impact of our individual actions is also seen in the "butterfly effect," which Princeton University defines as "the phenomenon whereby a small change at one place in a complex system can have large effects elsewhere." We need to remember that each new choice we make and every positive action we take has a profound effect on some aspect of our world.

Speaking with individuals and businesses across the globe, I realized that people truly want to both live more consciously and align their everyday actions with their personal values. They want to make educated consumer choices, live healthier, happier lives, and tread more lightly on the planet …but they don't always know where to start!

Start here. Each contributor profiled in this book represents a potential starting point or continuum on your personal journey. Contact those who inspire you, consult with them, talk to them and use them as springboards to discovery, self-empowerment and action. In doing so, you will ultimately enhance the lives of others and our planet as a whole.

Who is in the book?

Catalyst Publications invited applications from individuals, partnerships and businesses that represented their modality with integrity, experience, professionalism and dedication. We considered each of them through an interview and referral process. Although this is a comprehensive guide covering economic, social, environmental, community and personal issues, it is by no means exhaustive. There are many other unsung heroes doing exemplary work in these areas and we honour each and every one of them for their valuable contribution to our society.

On a personal note...

Many people are curious about how this book was born. It began with a nagging sense that I wasn't contributing enough to the world. I had been working internationally as a professional editorial and fine art photographer, with wonderful clients and no lack of adventure. But while I loved the creativity and expression involved, I felt that my work was not making a meaningful difference. History has shown that photography can be a significant catalyst in the world. But what was my angle?

Drawing from my background in marketing and my experience in holistic health and yoga, I observed a strong disconnect between the numerous options available for healthier, holistic living and the public's apparent reluctance to integrate these alternatives into their lives.

I spent months researching material, only to realize that what today's info-weary consumer requires is a distillation of the essential facts and options, presented in an accessible, distinctive way. I began to see how photography and storytelling could be used as an effective tool to enhance awareness of credible solutions. I founded Catalyst Publications in the hope that it would act as a portal to some of the most progressive thinkers and innovators of our times, and a catalyst for positive discussion and action.

It has been an honour to photograph and collaborate with the distinguished contributors featured in *Waking Up the West Coast: Healers and Visionaries*. Together, we have explored ideas, approaches, beliefs and visions that promote the healing of our bodies, minds, spirits, communities, environment and planet. I am inspired to continue to explore meaningful stories through the lens of my camera, and I hope that you, our valued reader, will be equally inspired by the people, words and images featured on these pages. I wish you great health, joy and fulfillment on your journey.

I invite you to send me your feedback about this book and to share any ideas or personal experiences you may have as a result of reading it.

To contact me, email: info@jaimekowal.com
To view my photography, visit: www.jaimekowal.com

"Every time you stand up for an ideal, you send forth a tiny ripple of hope."
– JOHN F. KENNEDY

Ambleside Beach, West Vancouver, British Columbia

CONTRIBUTORS

L-R: Karen Opas, Kaelan Wong, Sue Moen

A Loving Spoonful

Nourishment for those living with HIV/AIDS

"No one living with HIV or AIDS should also have to live with hunger," says Graeme Keirstead, president of A Loving Spoonful— a volunteer-driven, non-partisan society that provides free meals to people living with HIV in the Greater Vancouver area. By meeting the nutritional needs of those living with the virus, the society helps individuals improve their health and well-being so that they can focus on life's other challenges.

In its 17 years of operation, A Loving Spoonful has developed a model that incorporates harm-reduction strategies, personalized services and flexibility in meeting each client's needs and challenges. "Although we offer HIV-specific recipes and menus, emphasizing high-quality, organic and, where possible, local ingredients, it's the manner in which we deliver the meals that puts the 'Loving' in our name," says Keirstead. With 250 clients, the staff and volunteers can develop meaningful and empowering relationships with those they serve, helping them enhance their resistance to the virus through better health and nutrition. A Loving Spoonful also offers nutritional support services, such as education and skills building, nutritional counselling, and budgeting support.

Guided by its principles of non-discrimination, inclusiveness and flexibility, the society is leading a community partnership initiative to coordinate and enhance all food and nutrition services for the HIV-positive community. Their goal is to create a continuum of food-related services including free meal delivery, grocery hampers, congregate meals, community kitchens, coops/buying clubs, education, and skill-building and revenue-generating food security projects to increase individuals' self-reliance. "As catalysts for positive change, we envision a time when much of what we do can be done by, and for, the communities themselves," says Keirstead. "But we will continue to offer our knowledge and expertise to others working towards food security for all."

100 – 1300 Richards Street | Vancouver, BC | V6B 3G6 | **Contact:** Catherine Ewing
Tel: 604.682.6325 | **Fax:** 604.682.6327 | **Email:** info@alovingspoonful.org | **www.alovingspoonful.org**

Avalon Alliance Inc./Avalon Ecovillage Development Corporation

Laurel Zaseybida
Founder and President

The Avalon Alliance is dedicated to building the kind of life and community most people really want. Its founder, Laurel Zaseybida, is a sustainability planner promoting exciting approaches to green development and design that can transform cities, farms, homes and workplaces. Avalon's mission is to catalyze positive change and demonstrate powerful choices that lead to personal transformation and planetary renewal.

Working with an interdisciplinary team of innovative professionals from Canada, the United States and Europe, Zaseybida has launched an Ecovillage project in Kelowna that will achieve the highest international standards of energy efficiency and healthy living. The heart of this green residential development is an educational discovery centre offering services and workshops that address the wholeness of life. Visitors will be able to stay at this multicultural ecovillage and enjoy activities ranging from spiritual retreat and wellness workshops, to hands-on learning at an ecological design studio and solar-aquatic greenhouse.

Avalon Ecovillage is part of Zaseybida's larger vision of a model sustainability district, a "living-learning campus community for humanity." Her comprehensive master plan integrates sustainable urban housing and accommodation with extraordinary facilities for global studies, sacred arts, multimedia theatre, community health, interfaith fellowship, ethical commerce, eco-technology expo, children's education, organic horticulture and environmental stewardship. Avalon Alliance will undertake pioneering research, consulting outreach and leadership in holistic approaches and sustainable systems for the new millennium. It welcomes broad project participation, ranging from community members and professional associates to development partners and investors.

Zaseybida is also a spiritual healer who appreciates the interrelationships between the inner and outer worlds. "We must remember our divine potential as creative beings and boldly exercise our imagination and love, through authentic expression and living wholeheartedly," she says. "In order to thrive, we need a compelling vision and hope for the future, and Avalon is one such vision."

2 – 4025 Field Road | Kelowna, BC | V1W 4G1 | **Tel:** 250.868.8992 | **Fax:** 250.868.9368
Email: avalonalliance@shaw.ca | **www.avalonalliance.org**

13

Balance Within Coaching

Judy Bradshaw, RHN, RNCP
Registered Holistic Nutritionist, Touch for Health Practitioner, NLP Master Practitioner

Six years ago, when Judy Bradshaw was seeking answers to her health issues and experiencing very little support from the mainstream medical system, she found caring professionals with powerful alternative health methods—and unexpectedly discovered a new calling for herself. Wanting to learn those same modalities, Bradshaw immersed herself in studies at the Canadian School of Natural Nutrition and is now a Holistic Nutritionist, a Touch for Health Practitioner, and a Master Practitioner in Neuro-Linguistic Programming, serving clients who are experiencing chronic and often debilitating illnesses.

Bradshaw understands that mind and body are integrally connected and that they each contribute to good health, so she helps to heal her client's behavioural and emotional ailments. "Food alone does not nourish the physical body," she says. "Mind and consciousness also play a significant role. Emotions and behaviours can create false limitations on attainable goals; when unwanted emotions are cleared, you are left with a feeling of peace, joy and comfort."

Working one on one with her clients, Bradshaw uses non-invasive tools for assessing the body's needs, dislikes and energy mismatches and suggests tailored programs including healthy food choices that enable each person to reach and maintain optimal health. She provides helpful information on digestion, detoxification, assimilation and elimination. In addition, she creates a program to improve nutritional functions through the use of bio-therapeutic drainage, vitamins, minerals and trace elements, for example.

To help her clients change, adopt or eliminate behaviours such as depression, anger and fear, Bradshaw uses her skill as a Master Practitioner in Neuro-Linguistic Programming (NLP) and Time Linked Techniques. "Your unconscious mind has the blueprint of perfect health, and I help clients access that blueprint. Physical and emotional health is a gift we all deserve."

11574 – 83A Avenue | Delta, BC | V4C 2J8 | **Tel:** 604.599.4779
Fax: 604.599.6777 | **Email:** balancewithin@dccnet.com | **www.balancewithin.ca**

BARK Design Collective

Contributing to Canada's Cultural Currency

Dedicated to promoting Canadian design and innovation, the BARK Design Collective develops unique projects that introduce the world to a broader and more accurate display of Canadian culture while creating new economic opportunities for Canadians. BARK raises the profile of Canadian design through international exhibitions, publications and projects that are designed to be practical, provocative, informative, inspiring, engaging and seriously fun.

"We realized that Canada was being shortchanged by the widespread, limited stereotypes of what our country is and what it has to offer—maple syrup, raw logs and handsome Mounties," says Beth Hawthorn, one of BARK's six co-founders who, in 2002, committed to expanding those perceptions by showcasing Canada's innovative design talent. Since then, BARK has been enhancing Canada's reputation worldwide as a source of creative, high-quality design, promoting the idea of design as 'cultural currency' in Canada, and going where no Canadian design collective has gone before.

The All Terrain Cabin is a perfect example of the collective's innovative approach. A 480ft^2, fully outfitted design museum, it is self-contained, low-impact, smart, tough, cool and all Canadian. The fully transportable cabin unfolds to function as a contemporary shelter capable of supporting a family of four and a pet—while showcasing over 100 leading-edge examples of functionally and aesthetically superior Canadian innovations. With its sleek aluminum body and soft structured extensions, the All Terrain Cabin is equally at home at an international contemporary design forum, in the wilderness beside a lake, or atop a skyscraper. During the years leading up to the 2010 Olympic Games in Vancouver, the cabin will be sent on a world tour of design forums and premier events, demonstrating how we can live lightly on this earth. Appealing to consumers, business, design pros, environmental advocates and government officials alike, the exhibition is just one of BARK's contributions to a stronger, more competitive Canadian design industry—and a stronger, more competitive Canada.

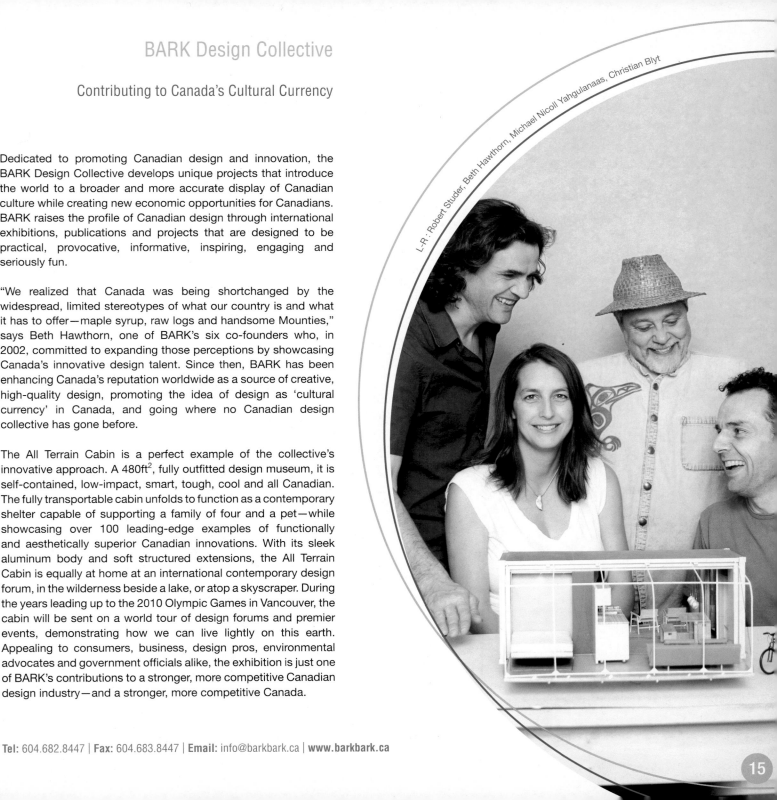

L-R: Robert Studer, Beth Hawthorn, Michael Nicoll Yahgulanaas, Christian Blyt

Tel: 604.682.8447 | **Fax:** 604.683.8447 | **Email:** info@barkbark.ca | **www.barkbark.ca**

Beyond the Waves Lodge & Spa

Taylore Sinclaire
Owner, Certified Watsu™ Practitioner,
Certified Ontological Coach

Nestled on the spectacular Sunshine Coast, Beyond the Waves Lodge & Spa is a luxurious retreat with sweeping vistas of the sea. Visitors at the Lodge can enjoy the serenity of the natural surroundings and the modern elegance of the beautiful accommodation, which includes a 1,200ft^2 suite. Offering unique spa treatments, such as Watsu and other forms of aquatic therapy, the Lodge is truly a sanctuary for healing, rest and rejuvenation.

Due to open in early 2007, the Lodge is the first of its kind in Canada. It is owned and operated by Taylore Sinclaire, a certified Watsu practitioner who also offers Water Dance, Jahara and Pre-natal Journey treatments, as well as Adaptive Watsu for those with special needs. Combining Zen Shiatsu techniques with warm-water therapy, her treatments blend the therapeutic benefits of 96° water with graceful and liberating movements, along with massage and Shiatsu point work. Clients experience expansion, softening and, ultimately, a deep sense of relaxation. "Floating during a bodywork session is a wonderfully liberating experience," says Sinclaire. "Clients can put aside everyday stresses and experience emotional safety and trust." In this state of peace, the treatment helps decrease chronic pain, reduce anxiety, improve sleep patterns, and may release suppressed emotions.

Sinclaire is creating a school associated with WABA—the Worldwide Aquatic Bodywork Association—and will hold regular aquatic bodywork classes at her Lodge. She is also an ontological coach, offering clients the opportunity to review and re-evaluate their response to, and memory of, past experiences. Sinclaire sees this as a natural complement to her Watsu treatments, which she often combines with coaching to help clients balance body, mind and spirit. "The highest reward for me is witnessing the transformation that occurs in my clients," says Sinclaire. "Stress lines disappear, muscles relax and years wash away. I call it the 'water facelift'."

6226 Sunshine Coast Highway | Sechelt, BC | V0N 3A7 | **Tel:** 604.885.WAVE (9283)
Cell: 604.612.3732 | **Fax:** 604.885.9285 | **Email:** waves@dccnet.com | **www.beyondthewavesspa.com**

Blue Energy Canada Inc.

Martin Burger
CEO

Victor Hugo claimed that there was nothing as powerful as an idea whose time had come. For Martin Burger, CEO of Blue Energy Canada Inc., tidal energy is that idea. One of the largest untapped sources of renewable energy, tidal power has the potential to generate electricity for most coastal communities, while enabling the planet to breathe easier. Burger plans to commercialize a new tidal power technology that will provide the world with low-cost sustainable energy—with numerous economic, social and ecological benefits. Using advanced aerospace technology, Blue Energy's ocean turbines generate efficient, renewable and emission-free electricity at prices competitive with today's conventional energy sources.

Born of Cree heritage and raised in the Canadian subarctic, Burger worked as a diamond driller in the mining camps of Canada's far north to put himself through his civil engineering studies, graduating with distinction from the Northern Alberta Institute of Technology. Influenced by Dene elders who helped raise him, he is a strong advocate for a viable, environmentally sustainable future. His tidal energy solution is independent of weather and climate change, relying on ocean currents rather than tidal amplitude to generate electricity. Acting as highly efficient underwater 'windmills', Blue Energy's ocean turbines have a simple design that requires no new construction methodology and is economical to build, install and maintain.

The Blue Energy technology will enable communities to generate electricity without emitting greenhouse gases or damaging the local marine environment. With worldwide electricity consumption predicted to double over the next 20 years, and almost two billion people currently without electrical power, Blue Energy offers a sustainable, ethical and planet-friendly energy solution that can simultaneously reduce the world's reliance on fossil fuels. An idea whose time has come? "The writing's on the wall," says Burger. "Tidal power is the wave of the future."

Tel: 604.408.2508 | **Email:** ceo@bluenergy.com | **www.bluenergy.com**

L-R: Luke Balson, Don Wong

Camp Moomba

Don Wong, Executive Director
Luke Balson, Program Director

Established in 1997, Camp Moomba is a specialized summer camp program for kids aged six to seventeen dealing with HIV/AIDS. Many of the children attending the camp share similar issues in their lives, such as difficult socio-economic situations. By coming together each year at the camp, they are able to find the type of support that comes from understanding. Camp Moomba is a place where campers experience a community based on equality, friendship and support. Its name—and the foundation of the camp's philosophy—is inspired by the Australian aboriginal word that means 'friends together having fun.' Run by the YMCA and funded by the Western Canadian Pediatric AIDS Society, Camp Moomba is unique in Canada.

"Every day, our kids live in difficult situations because of the stigma of HIV," says Camp Executive Director Don Wong. "Many feel isolated, unable to share the full impact of how the disease affects their lives." At Camp Moomba each summer, HIV-impacted children are brought together from across Canada and are reunited with other campers and counsellors, sharing smiles, laughter and stories in the context of a shared understanding of living with HIV. It's a chance to see old friends from camp, meet some new ones, and a chance to just be kids.

The camp is committed to fostering leadership development among the campers through its teen leadership program. Participants work together in safe, yet challenging, activities, learning how to instruct and guide others to success in all areas around camp. It is a fulfilling opportunity that allows participants to demonstrate and strengthen their skills in self-discipline and in taking initiative. Camp Moomba's exceptional program, in the spirit of equality, is offered cost-free. Truly, it is a place for belonging.

223 – 119 West Pender Street | Vancouver, BC | V6B 1S4 | Tel: 604.684.1701
Fax: 604.684.1741 | Email: info@campmoomba.com | www.campmoomba.com

Capers Community Markets

Certified Organic Retailer

Trista Swaby

In 1985, a group of forward-thinking West Coasters got together around a shared belief—that a modern grocery store ought to make a positive contribution to the well-being of its community. Now with three Vancouver area stores joining the West Vancouver original, Capers Community Markets continues to redefine the neighbourhood market experience with its decidedly unconventional approach—one that attracts many like-minded people.

To help encourage healthy eating, Capers employs an in-house nutritionist, and has an advisory group including some of the region's leading integrated health professionals. In peak season, from August to October, nearly 80% of Capers' produce is local and organic supplied by a network of over 30 farmers and growers. In February 2006, Capers became the first Canadian retailer to be certified organic by Quality Assurance International (QAI). Some other firsts include the removal of products containing hydrogenated oils from their shelves and exclusive use of fair-trade sugar in its in-store baking.

Though rooted in the natural and organic food movement, the Capers team is a regular, active supporter of other innovative and effective community organizations. It also produces its own events aimed at building a strong community of socially conscious consumers advocating healthy change, while savouring all the benefits this region offers. Perhaps the most popular example is Capers' annual Living Naturally Fair, an autumn weekend celebration of fresh, healthy food and fun that has, in the past decade, also raised more than $300,000 for such social and environmental initiatives as Camp Moomba, A Loving Spoonful, the YWCA and the Vancouver Aquarium's Ocean Wise program.

Building personal, loyal relationships with its local suppliers, community partners and, naturally, customers, is more than just Capers' core mission. It's what nourishes them.

Regional Office, 2285 West 4th Avenue, 2nd Floor | Vancouver, BC | V6K 1N9
Tel: 604.739.6640 | Fax: 604.739.6649 | Email: info@capersmarkets.com | www.capersmarkets.com

Change Advertising

Marc Stoiber
Founder

Change Advertising is a green-brand marketing incubator—specializing in making sustainable brands famous, sustainable companies successful, and sustainability sexy. Founded by award-winning advertising creative director Marc Stoiber, Change caters to the growing number of clients who see a disconnect between their values and their everyday consumer decisions. Change's priorities have evolved accordingly: clients must believe that advertising works; their products/services have to be competitive with those of mainstream companies; and the company must be doing something to make the world a better place. "In our opinion, there's far too much talk in the sustainability game and not nearly enough action," says Stoiber. "We hope to change that by convincing conscious consumers to buy into forward-thinking brands."

Key to the process are 'ThinkChange' sessions with clients that look at all facets of the brand. These sessions involve all of the client company's human-resource levels—from the president to the people handling complaint calls. "These sessions yield incredible brand stories and facilitate breakthrough thinking," says Stoiber.

Staffed with senior, award-winning talent from the mainstream marketing world, Change offers clients top-flight thinking and experience, and saves them a steep learning curve. "We're like plutonium—we aren't inexpensive, but our thinking is concentrated and very, very effective," he says. "That enables us to get to the point faster and create more effective brand communication."

Stoiber's motivation is both professional and personal. "I have a little boy—and that means I need to do my part to clean up our world."

2769 West 1st Avenue | Vancouver, BC | V6K 1H2 | **Tel:** 604.738.8080
Email: marc@changeadvertising.com | **www.changeadvertising.com**

Christine Sui-Yee Hwang

Visual Artist, Graphic Designer, Traditional Chinese Feng Shui Practitioner

Christine Sui-Yee Hwang fuses her life experience, education, philosophy and talent into her multimedia creative practice, which includes drawing, painting, printmaking, photography, graphic design and traditional Chinese feng shui. She is a graduate of the Emily Carr Institute of Art and Design and studies under the guidance of her mother, Teresa Hwang, a senior practitioner and lecturer for Master Joseph Yu's Feng Shui Research Centre. "I try to always keep an open dialogue between my art, design and feng shui practices," she says. "Feng shui is a very beneficial art form as it affects one's happiness and well-being in a precise way. I also believe that, since all things are interconnected, this open approach is the healthiest and most natural way to work."

Hwang is also actively engaged in her community. Due to early experiences with racial discrimination, Hwang became involved with human rights and social justice activities. She volunteered for the North Okanagan Youth Race Relations Committee and Reaching Across Differences. She also helped organize and facilitate anti-racism youth forums and conferences. Along with her freelance work, Hwang volunteers her multimedia talents to charities such as Nalandabodhi Canada and Lotus Speech. In keeping with her commitment to social justice, her highest aspiration is enabling sustainable peace.

She believes that each of us can work towards eliminating all forms of aggression and violence in the world. "If we could care for others as if they were our own family then no one would experience poverty, famine, a lack of education and healthcare, war, crime, abuse or exploitation," says Hwang. Her work with clients reflects this passionate commitment to a healthy, happy and conscious life.

8509 Laurel Street | Vancouver, BC | V6P 3V4 | **Tel:** 604.321.0608
Cell: 778.888.0205 | **Email:** art.media@christinehwang.ca | www.christinehwang.ca

L-R: Beth Hawthorn, Leslie Grant

CORE - Vancouver's Natural Living Guide

Beth Hawthorn and Leslie Grant
Founders

CORE is a unique 'healthy-lifestyle' guide created by two passionate Vancouverites, Beth Hawthorn and Leslie Grant. It is an annotated directory of Vancouver's growing health and wellness communities, featuring progressive local companies committed to positive growth and change. The annual guide includes over $6,000 worth of coupons for popular eco-friendly, healthy products and services, including yoga and Pilates, organic foods, clothing, travel, retreats, books, gifts, spas and more. "Our mandate is to promote the ideals of wellness and sustainability, as well as the businesses that do the same in our neighbourhoods," says Grant. "The CORE directory puts you in touch with the abundance of companies that take health, environmental and social responsibilities as seriously as you do."

Shopping from the CORE directory helps consumers to not only make conscious choices about the products and services they purchase, but also support the local economy. Using Core Passes (coupons) enables individuals to try out the various services and products offered in the guide. "The most rewarding thing about our work is meeting the people actively involved in promoting health and wellness, as well as those seeking a better lifestyle for themselves, their families and the community," says Hawthorn.

Several schools and non-profit organizations are selling copies of CORE as part of their fundraising campaigns. By doing so, they become part of CORE's network of support for local responsible businesses and the building of a healthier community. Requiring only a small investment that yields a high rate of return, the guide provides fundraisers with something that is easy to sell and that is worthwhile for the whole family. CORE also contains informative articles on healthy, natural and organic living, with lots of tips and snippets on community activities, environmental awareness, global peace initiatives and other healthy lifestyle options.

Tel: 604.874.9642 | Email: info@corebook.ca | **www.corebook.ca**

Creative Sublime Lifestyles™

Sheryl Ann Fitzharris
Lifestyle Facilitator, Public Speaker, Entrepreneur

"There are two significant moments in our lives: one is when we are born, the other is when we find out why." Sheryl Fitzharris knows why she is here: she is committed to the empowerment of her clients through nutritional health and effective personal financial management. Through her company, Creative Sublime Lifestyles, she offers personal consultations to both individuals and groups, with her popularity as a keynote speaker enabling her to share her insights with large audiences. "My passion is inspiring others to reconnect with their dreams, and to incorporate financial exit strategies and a dynamic mentorship program that offers the opportunity to gain greater health, wealth and enjoyment in their lives," she says.

She believes that the key to assisting and empowering others is to begin by identifying their personal and financial goals. "The hectic world of today has people forgetting their dreams, passions and inherent ability to achieve whatever they wish," says Fitzharris. She mentors clients as they work to realize their objectives using the opportunity available through Sunrider International. For nearly a quarter of a century, Sunrider International has been a global leader in creating financial independence and wellness with over 400 awarding-winning products now available in 40 countries around the world. Fitzharris was introduced to this visionary company over 18 years ago and it has become her vehicle for creating her ideal lifestyle.

Fitzharris believes "when a person's body is nourished with whole food nutrition, their body and mind vibrate at a higher level, where inner strength, hope, passion and purpose come to light and become an everyday experience." She has achieved great success with Sunrider International, both for herself and for her clients. She is an Independent Distributor, Silver Master Director and a highly regarded member of the Sunrider advisory board.

236 – 1628 West 1st Avenue | Vancouver, BC | V6J 1G1 | Tel: 604.739.8408
Cell: 778.883.5300 | Email: sfitzharris@telus.net | www.creativesublime.com

23

D'Alton's Bio-Energy Therapy

Michael D'Alton
Architect of D'Alton's Bio-Energy Therapy,
Director, International School of Energy Medicine

Michael D'Alton is the Director of the International School of Energy Medicine. The school specializes in pain management using his D'Alton's Bio-Energy Therapy—a system of specialized manual treatments—to help clients recover from conditions such as back pain, migraines and arthritis. "I feel that our response to events occurring in our life is our responsibility. Accepting this responsibility is empowering and this is the point at which we can create great change in our lives," he says.

Bio-Energy Therapy, which is non-invasive and suitable for all ages, has been featured internationally for its remarkable success in treating chronic ailments. Many health professionals have found incorporating the teachings and tools complementary to their own professional practice. Bio-Energy Therapy acts as a catalyst to redirect one's focus and energy away from sickness and towards greater health and well-being. Many clients feel the benefits of this relaxing treatment immediately, and experience positive, long-term results. In his therapeutic practice, D'Alton addresses blockages in the bio-energy field, the electro-magnetic energy flowing through and around the body. Each session involves scanning this field to determine the location and causes of blockages, the removal of these blockages, and balancing and energizing the field enabling the client to achieve a higher level of vibration. "Through my work, I have discovered that our intentions, ideas, thoughts and feelings shape our reality and experience," says D'Alton. "I train my clients to choose their thoughts and intentions more consciously."

D'Alton teaches a unique nine-month diploma program that leads students through seven personal and spiritual steps to become professional Bio-Energy Therapists. He also provides ongoing professional support and development to his practitioners.

540 – 1755 Robson Street | Vancouver, BC | V6G 3B7
Tel: 604.638.5175 | Email: info@daltonsbio.com | www.daltonsbio.com

Danielle McDermott, MA

Psychotherapist,
Certified Yoga Therapist and Teacher

As a yoga therapist with a Masters Degree in Psychology, Danielle McDermott's goal is to empower clients to better understand themselves, their feelings and the connection between their minds and bodies in a holistic way. Her unique approach combines traditional talk therapy with gentle yoga poses and breathing techniques to create a holistic treatment for mind and body. The yoga poses are specifically selected based on the client's issues and are designed to complement and deepen emotional release while promoting subsequent healing.

"Our thoughts affect our bodies and our entire way of being in this life," says McDermott. "Increasing self-awareness, learning to listen to the subtle messages from our bodies and developing the ability to choose how we think and feel can be transformational, liberating and deeply healing." She believes that her clients are their own experts and that her role is to show them how to access the wisdom within. "Yoga therapy works because clients learn to take responsibility for their own health and recognize that healing is a personal choice," she says. "Too often we turn to professionals to 'heal us' and forget that we must be 100% committed to the process and actively involved mentally and physically in creating the change we want in our lives. Many of the answers we almost compulsively search for outside ourselves can be answered from within by simply learning to listen to the messages the body and mind are giving us. This is usually not a quick fix, but rather a more sincere, profound and lasting solution."

McDermott advocates proper breathing, from the stomach rather than the chest, as a basic skill that can have immediate positive benefits, especially when combined with visualization techniques. On the inhale, breathe in relaxation; on the exhale, breathe out tension and feel your body becoming ever more relaxed and peaceful.

Vitality Clinic | 827 Hamilton Street | Vancouver, BC | V6B 2R7
Tel: 604.687.7678 | **Email:** danielle@mindbodyhealing.ca | **www.mindbodyhealing.ca**

Dr Jim Chan Naturopathic Clinic

Dr Jim Chan, ND
Naturopathic Physician, Acupuncturist

Like the ancient healers in China, India, Greece and in Native American cultures, Dr Jim Chan works with patients to identify the root cause of their illness and offer a holistic approach to support body, mind and soul through the healing process. A naturopathic physician since 1989, Dr Chan specializes in chronic metabolic diseases, including cancer and cardiovascular disease. Completing his biochemistry degree, Dr Chan was inspired to explore different forms of medicine and how the human body works, which led him to embrace the true essence of naturopathy—which literally means 'nature heals.'

Dr Chan arrived in Canada with the goal of completing medical school. After training for two years in medical laboratory technology, he segued into naturopathic medicine, while still working as a laboratory technician in a local hospital. As a result, his private practice is fully equipped with cutting-edge diagnostic instruments. The clinic can perform chelation and other bio-oxidative therapies. Using treatments based on the body's innate ability to fight disease and heal itself, Dr Chan also works with anti-aging and longevity medicine, complementary cancer care and prevention, acupuncture, weight management, colon therapy, allergy testing and detoxification programs.

Dr Chan is a firm believer in the importance of stimulating the body's intrinsic powers of healing, rather than bombarding patients with prescriptions for pharmaceutical drugs and surgery. "We thrive on seeking new treatments that are safe and effective," he says. "Technologies in medicine are out there to help just about any disorder we could possibly think of. It's just a matter of seeking them out and applying them."

He is currently in the process of developing wellness and prevention programs for his patients. It is his vision that brought about the Gift of Life Foundation—a non-profit organization that will provide financial assistance to qualified patients.

3331 No. 3 Road | Richmond, BC | V6X 2B6 | **Tel:** 604.273.4372
Cell: 604.789.1818 | **Fax:** 604.303.9663 | **Email:** info@drjimchan.com | **www.drjimchan.com**

Echo Valley Ranch and Spa

Norm and Nanthawon Dove
Owners

At Echo Valley Ranch and Spa, guests enjoy a spectacular western adventure in a superb sanctuary of first-class accommodations, healthy gourmet food, complete spa services, and a diverse choice of enriching outdoor recreational activities, all set within the breathtaking landscape. Norm and Nanthawon Dove were awed by the serenity and beauty of the land when they first visited the area. "We were overwhelmed by a sense of spirituality and reverence for it. To this day, we still cannot describe the feeling— it's simply beyond words."

Echo Valley Ranch and Spa is one of Canada's premier guest ranches. Here, the spirit of the West is combined with a uniquely Asian feel in its architecture, hospitality and spa treatments. The Cariboo Spa offers classic European treatments and refinement services: facials, hydrotherapy, body scrubs, manicures and hair care, to name just a few. The Thai Spa is based on the ancient wisdom of traditional Thai medicine; therapies include Thai massage, Thai foot massage and the Luk Pra Kob hot compress treatment. Echo Valley's signature spa experience, Sabai Sabai, incorporates some treatments similar to those enjoyed by Thailand's royal family, and are provided in the ranch's magnificent Baan Thai spa pavilion, the only such spa in North America. Sabai Sabai is a Thai phrase for an all-encompassing feeling of well-being, to embrace a holistic state of contentment. At Echo Valley, the Sabai Sabai experience is a way of life.

The Echo Valley Ranch and Spa experience inspires healthy living. "We encourage guests to incorporate spa treatments into their daily lives and help them understand the importance of exercise, food choices and meditation," say the Doves. With horseback riding, hiking, fly fishing, birding and more, there is something to suit everyone's interest. Echo Valley Ranch and Spa offers a getaway for singles, couples and business professionals alike, attracting visitors from around the world.

L-R: Norm and Nanthawon Dove

PO Box 16, Clinton | Jesmond, BC | V0K 1K0 | Tel: 250.459.2386 | Fax: 250.459.0086
Reservations: 1.800.253.8831 | Email: info@evranch.com | www.evranch.com

Elite Earth-friendly Cleaners

Laurel and Rick Nathorst
Owners and Operators

A family business dedicated to providing the finest garment care, Elite Earth-friendly Cleaners is a solvent-free, green alternative to ordinary dry cleaning. Rather than immersing garments in toxic chemicals that emit harmful gases, they use nature's best solvent: water. Their natural cleaning processes pose no risk to their staff, their customers or the planet—plus clothes are cleaner, smell better and last longer with their state-of-the-art European system. Elite specializes in wedding gowns, vintage restorations and difficult-to-clean garments.

Owners Rick Nathorst and his wife, Laurel, switched to the eco-friendly system in 2003 after Laurel was diagnosed with advanced ovarian cancer. "It compelled us to examine our deepest values. We shifted our focus from merely making a living to making our life and our business deeply satisfying." The Nathorsts became actively involved in trying to change the world by using their business as a vehicle for charity, social justice and environmental work. They helped other cleaners 'go green' and are responsible for cruise-ship giant Holland America using the same non-toxic system on dozens of their ships. They also created Winter Warmth, a charity campaign for which they collected, cleaned and distributed over two tonnes of clothing for the homeless and disadvantaged.

Elite has won numerous awards for its work in pollution prevention and sustainability, including a Vancity Ethics in Action award in 2005 and an Eco-Star Award given by the Capital Regional District for outstanding contributions in sustainable business practice. In 2006, the Nathorsts won a Canadian Council of Ministers of the Environment award for their innovation and leadership in preventing pollution. "We love the fact that our contributions have been recognized, but the truth is we're grateful to effect positive change in the world, and we would do it anyway because we believe that our business should be a reflection of our spirits."

1019 Cook Street | Victoria, BC | V8V 3Z6 | **Tel:** 250.381.2221
Email: earthfriendly@shaw.ca | **www.greendrycleaner.com**

Envision Sustainability Tools Inc.

Dave Biggs
Co-founder, Software Developer, Facilitator,
Futurist, Sustainability Visionary

What if there were an interactive tool that could evaluate future scenarios, facilitate the creation of sustainable visions, and promote smarter planning? Would decision-makers use it to create sustainable communities? They already do, according to Dave Biggs, co-creator of MetroQuest, an award-winning computer simulation tool that has been dubbed 'the real-life SimCity'. MetroQuest shows how our environmental, social and economic conditions can be simultaneously improved. But MetroQuest is more than just software; it's a proven approach for urban and regional planning that turns stakeholders into constructive partners.

"One critical aspect of MetroQuest is its ability to help communities look at the long-term consequences of their choices and to see the full lifecycle impact of decisions played out over several decades," says Biggs, who developed the software with Dr John Robinson and other researchers at UBC. "Many of the most critical choices relating to sustainability are those made at the community level— where we live, where we work, how we get around and what we consume. My vision is to create cities that behave less like factories and more like ecosystems, where balance, synergies, efficiency and regeneration are built into the design and seem to happen effortlessly."

The approach has been used successfully to move communities, cities and whole regions on four continents towards a more sustainable future. Working with communities worldwide, Biggs makes the process fun, interactive and highly visual. Participants are rewarded with meaningful information about the long-range consequences of their choices; they finish with a shared vision for a more sustainable community, informed by diverse perspectives. "When we can deeply engage a large enough portion of the community that the new vision becomes part of the DNA of the place," says Biggs, "positive change is not only possible, it's inevitable!"

300 – 1 Alexander Street | Vancouver, BC | V6A 1B2 | **Tel:** 604.225.2010 | **Cell:** 604.317.6200
Fax: 604.225.2001 | **Email:** daveb@envisiontools.com | **www.questforthefuture.com**

equine-imity™

Linda-Ann Bowling
Founder, Director, Intuitive Healing Coach

Early in her childhood, Linda-Ann Bowling heard a calling to serve the world by helping others to find their passion and life purpose. She answered her call in an unusual way, with the assistance of some surprising teachers and healers—horses. "The belief systems that cause us to get stuck can be transformed through listening and connecting with the highly intuitive wisdom of horses," says Bowling. "I believe that horses 'called me' to guide individuals in their quest to find their own personal power and to create major shifts in their lives."

Bowling is the founder and director of equine-imity™. Her enterprise is part of Planned Transitions, a collective whose purpose, programs and workshops bring people closer to discovering their authentic selves, resolving issues and creating sustainable change. "The horse has been a symbol of power and strength for thousands of years and, today, horses offer us a partnership for learning built on authenticity, intention, courage, intuition and focus," she explains. "Our horses are willing co-facilitators in our journey of learning and self-discovery, and take us to unimaginable depths of wisdom."

equine-imity™ offers a number of developmental, professional and personal growth programs for adults, couples and teens, as well as corporate and business programs including leadership and team development, conflict resolution, relationship-building and assertiveness training. Bowling is also the author and designer of *Soul Spa*™, a program and learning guide written for women which teaches seven essential life practices for building joy, balance and fulfillment.

Bowling's values of integrity, trust, respect and collaboration are integral to her work with both horses and humans. "Through my work, I am healed. I believe that we were meant to walk together in harmony, grace and lightness. The horses help us to remember the lightness."

25027 Robertson Crescent | Langley, BC | V4W 1W7 | **Tel:** 604.626.4806 | **Cell:** 604.889.4452
Fax: 604.626.4807 | **Email:** linda-ann@equine-imity.com | **www.equine-imity.com** | **www.soulspa.ca**

Dr Erica Reznick

Registered Clinical Psychologist,
Poet, Collaborative Law Divorce Coach,
Vice-Chair of the Garbha Institute

Bring your precious stories
by the hand
and,
together,
we will marry your lessons
with wisdom.

Dr Erica Reznick's therapeutic work with individuals, couples and families, as a Registered Clinical Psychologist and a collaborative law divorce coach, has spanned over 20 years. Drawing from a wide range of therapeutic modalities, she approaches each client holistically, addressing the cognitive, emotional, social and spiritual dynamics of change and experience. "I work towards change that is both uniquely defined and multifaceted for each individual." Dr Reznick comes to the field of collaborative work with a passion for facilitating "kind divorce," helping couples and children navigate separation in the safest and most compassionate manner possible. She also teaches the practice of mindful parenting and the emotional competencies that accompany it.

When discussing her work with clients, Dr Reznick emphasizes the value and respect she has for the courage it takes to create change. "Sometimes the most difficult crises that leave us feeling bereft and victimized are the very experiences that contain the seeds of change—of powerful growth and transcendence of a life lesson." Her healing focus centres on empowerment—helping individuals and families to make better life choices, to understand the intergenerational patterns of life lessons, and to live daily with conscious intent.

Speak to Dr Reznick and it is instantly apparent that she is following her passion: "I have the opportunity to continually develop deep empathy and compassion for others through my work, to cultivate authenticity in relationships each and every day. When clients gift me with the honour of being their guide and witness, my heart is infused."

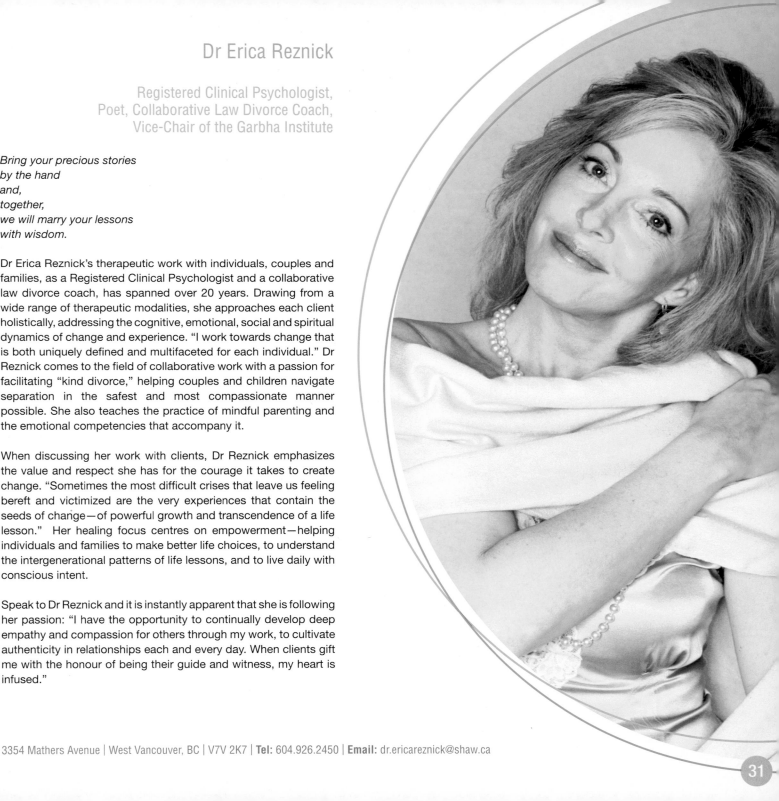

Espiritu Healing Arts Centre

Siobhan O'Connell
Founder, Registered Physiotherapist, Clinical Director

Siobhan O'Connell's vision is to bring state-of-the-art Physical Medicine—assessment, treatment and education—to her patients in a serene, peaceful environment. The Espiritu Healing Arts Centre adheres to the Integrated Medicine model that recognizes the natural healing capacity of all human beings and the important role the health of spirit and mind plays in relation to the health of the physical body. To support this vision and facilitate the client's achievement of individual health goals, Espiritu boasts a full spectrum of highly experienced health professionals who are ready to help each client identify and meet their own specific targets.

Physiotherapy is the axis around which all other modalities are planned and integrated. Each client's personal treatment plan may also include Registered Massage Therapy, Traditional Chinese Medicine, acupuncture, and rehabilitation exercise with a special focus on Pilates and therapeutic yoga. A Transpersonal Psychotherapist teaches weekly Modern Meditation classes and is available for individual consultations, as required. "We believe that brokering relationships between our clients and an experienced team of health professionals provides our clients with a continuum of dedicated care and communication," says O'Connell, Espiritu's clinical director. "We are passionate about empowering our clients through the treatment process and beyond." Espiritu provides ongoing programs, education and links to the integrated medicine field, helping clients to be the best possible stewards of their own health at every age and stage.

As an Integrated Medicine practitioner, O'Connell cares deeply about treating wholly through the mind, body and spirit connection. This model represents the next level in the evolution of healthcare. It is being validated scientifically around the world. O'Connell ensures that all therapists and referring physicians are in regular communication to streamline the client's experience. Espiritu ensures that patients feel genuinely cared for by offering them loving and expert attention.

202 – 106 West 1st Street | North Vancouver, BC | V7M 2A6 | **Tel:** 604.982.0366
Fax: 604.982.9365 | **Email:** siobhan@espiritu.ca | **www.espiritu.ca**

Essential Health Natural Medicine Clinic

Dr Cobi Slater, DNM, CHT
Doctor of Natural Medicine, Clinical Therapist, Natural Health Consultant/Technician/Educator

Thomas Edison claimed that the doctor of the future would give no medicine, but would interest the patient in the care of the human frame, in diet and in the cause and prevention of disease. Sharing this philosophy, Dr Cobi Slater has dedicated herself to the practice of natural medicine, offering a variety of alternative modalities for mental, physical and emotional well-being. With extensive training in naturopathy, natural medicine, clinical herbal therapy and health education, Dr Slater offers complementary healthcare services for all age groups through her Essential Health Natural Medicine Clinic.

The clinic addresses chronic disease, immune disorders, allergies, skin problems and digestive complaints, providing nutritional, lifestyle and weight-management counselling, as well as laboratory testing for hormonal imbalances, bone density, breast cancer and heavy metals. It also specializes in women's health, pregnancy and babies, offering special kits for newborns, pregnancy and stress, each containing several different natural remedies. As a compounding herbalist, Dr Slater has the added advantage of being able to compound unique formulas to meet her patients' individual needs. "Knowing that we have nearly every medicine we need growing in the earth was what prompted me to choose natural medicine," she says. "I knew that I could help people heal naturally—not just in my office, but anywhere at any time."

Extending far beyond her office, Dr Slater's services include extensive medical missionary work throughout the countries of Central America and online or telephone consultations for patients around the world. Her approach to health is equally without borders, as she believes that all forms of medicine have a place in healing. "Whether it is natural or conventional, our focus is to work together to improve the health of the patient and integration is the key to optimal health."

24188 Hill Avenue | Maple Ridge, BC | V2W 2E1
Tel: 604.828.9594 | **Email:** cshealth@telus.net | **www.drcobi.com**

33

The Ethical Funds Company®

Elaine McHarg
Senior Vice-President and Chief Marketing Officer

For Canadians who place a high priority on socially responsible investment strategies, The Ethical Funds Company is the perfect financial partner. With two decades of experience in sustainable investing, and offering Canada's most comprehensive family of sustainable investment options, Ethical Funds® provides professional investment management that reflects the environmental, social, and governance values of its investors.

The Ethical Funds Company believes that sustainable investing is about more than simply investing in good companies—it is about making good companies better. "We believe that companies can prosper by adopting sustainable business practices by treating employees well, by maintaining good community relations, by being sensitive to environmental impacts, and by becoming more accountable to society," says senior vice-president, Elaine McHarg.

Through its integrated Sustainable Investing Program, Ethical Funds encourages businesses to become more sustainable by engaging them in dialogue on environmental, social and governance issues. Their Corporate Sustainability Scorecard employs between 55 and 120 indices across 34 sectors to objectively assess a company's social and environmental performance. They actively seek out companies that promote progressive stakeholder relations, equal opportunities and exemplary environmental practices. Both financial performance and sustainable performance are core values for Ethical Funds as they implement strategies aimed at helping businesses become better corporate citizens.

The Ethical Funds Company is proud of its service and commitment to communities, with profits flowing back to the credit unions in the communities where their funds are sold. Investors with Ethical Funds are helping to build a more sustainable world. They have the satisfaction of creating personal financial security knowing their investments are making a positive difference in the global community.

800 – 1111 West Georgia Street | Vancouver, BC | V6E 4T6 | **Contact:** Jane Mitchell, Public Relations
Tel: 604.714.3800 | **Fax:** 604.714.3861 | **Email:** jmitchell@ethicalfunds.com | **www.ethicalfunds.com**
Ethical Funds® and The Ethical Funds Company are registered marks owned by Ethical Funds Inc.

Expression

Angela Roy
Presenter, Educator, Performing Artist

"Through the pathways of rhythmic and vocal arts, we celebrate community!" exclaims Angela Roy. By bringing people together through movement, dance and song, Roy instills a sense of well-being, inspiration and empowerment through her dynamic workshops and performances. Whether she is working with children, youth or professionals, "each experience brings a sense of value and meaning. The arts build healthy communities and promote collective joy." The founder of the interactive performing arts company, Expression, Roy is a dancer, singer and percussionist and has designed the Rhythmic Art! Program, which provides participants of all ages and abilities with an interactive experience of music and culture through storytelling, movement activities and an eclectic combination of world and African beats and songs. It offers a unique experience of dance fusion, chants and percussion performances and workshops, where participants are encouraged to play with the provided drums and instruments.

Roy, who tours throughout Western Canada, is known for her high energy and her ability to connect with people, whether she is working as an artist in the classroom, performing at cultural-recreation events, presenting at professional development conferences or to corporate clients. In addition to her workshops and performances, Roy has developed the *Collective Creativity* instructional CD for teachers, and has co-recorded *The Tambour Moving Arts Project Children's World Music* CD for kids of all ages.

Roy's gift is her dynamic presence, enthusiasm and passion for the arts. Her focus is on empowering people and she inspires them to embrace the notion that "if you can walk, you can dance, if you can talk, you can sing, and if you can say the rhythm, you can play the rhythm!"

1606 30th Street | Vernon, BC | V1T 5E8 | **Cell:** 250.212.7594
Email: angela@expression.bc.ca | **www.expression.bc.ca**

Feng Shui Your Life

Suzette Laqua, BA, CFSP
Founder and President

According to the Eastern art of feng shui (pronounced *fung shway*), how we arrange our rooms and furniture has a profound effect on our psychological and spiritual well-being. This ancient Chinese art holds that arranging one's environment into certain harmonious patterns can bring a sense of abundance, balance and happiness. Feng shui is about honouring ourselves and having the intention to create an atmosphere that is specific to our needs and desires that will give back in the most positive way. By applying the principles of this art, it is possible to make our living and working environments healthier and more attuned to the life forces that surround us.

Suzette Laqua, founder and president of Feng Shui Your Life, and Certified Feng Shui Practitioner, earned her Bachelor of Arts degree in Psychology from Simon Fraser University. She combines the Eastern (feng shui) and Western (psychology) philosophies and principles to encourage and guide people through obstacles in their lives. Laqua believes that "by honouring ourselves and creating more harmony in our life and environment, everyone will experience greater fulfillment."

Laqua's love of helping people, combined with her passion for interior decorating, brings balance and joy into the lives of her clients. "I help, encourage and inspire individuals to make the necessary changes in their environments, helping balance and harmonize their lives." When she uses feng shui in the homes, offices and businesses of clients, they see, feel and live the positive changes that surround them. "There is a definite need to 'Feng Shui Your Life' in order to create harmony, safety and more productive living and working environments." As a registered member of the International Feng Shui Guild, Laqua is available to speak to groups of any size, teach classes and conduct weekend workshops.

813 6th Street | New Westminster, BC | V3L 3C8 | **Tel:** 778.772.8495
Email: suzette@fengshuiyourlife.ca | **www.fengshuiyourlife.ca**

ForestEthics

Tzeporah Berman
Founder and Program Director

Only three countries in the world—Canada, Russia and Brazil—have enough forest left to maintain biodiversity, which, ecologically speaking, is critically important to the development of all living species. In Canada, five acres' worth of trees are logged every minute. When Tzeporah Berman learned about this bleak situation, she took immediate action and founded ForestEthics, a non-profit environmental organization whose mission is the protection of endangered forests. The corporate power that destroys forests, she discovered, could be used to protect the 'lungs' of planet Earth. To date, ForestEthics has saved over seven million acres. "Knowing that rainforest valleys from Canada to Chile have been protected forever is incredibly rewarding," says Berman. "And working with individuals who are motivated to make change, from First Nations to corporate purchasing officers, is inspiring."

ForestEthics was one of the primary negotiators of the Great Bear Rainforest agreement that ensured the permanent protection of five million acres of rainforest on British Columbia's coast. That negotiation process helped to forge a new collegial alliance between government, First Nations, environmental groups and industry that will continue to serve the province of BC. ForestEthics is also a leader of the campaign to ensure that major corporations, such as Staples and Office Depot, use their buying power to protect forests.

The current goal of ForestEthics is twofold: it is committed to the protection of millions of acres of endangered forest including BC's Clayoquot Sound and the inland temperate rain forests of Canada, the United States and Chile; the organization is also dedicated to bringing about a dramatic shift in the marketplace towards the consumption of ecologically responsible wood and paper products. "The fact that some of our last great forests are being destroyed to make catalogues and newspapers is a travesty," says Berman. "We are responsible in this era not only for what we do but also for what we do not do."

604 – 850 West Hastings | Vancouver, BC | V6C 1E1 | **Tel:** 604.331.6201
Fax: 604.408.7210 | **Email:** tzeporah@forestethics.org | **www.forestethics.ca**

37

Free To Be™ Rehab Consulting

Barbara Purdy, Registered Physical and Occupational Therapist, Ergonomics Advisor, Workshop Developer and Facilitator, Master Reiki Practitioner

Barbara Purdy is a crusader for safety in the workplace. Her professional physiotherapy and occupational therapy experiences, personal history, and ergonomics background have helped her to create individualized health and safety training programs and workshops that prevent and reduce work-related injuries. Purdy works closely with businesses to establish ergonomically designed offices and workstations; implements 'no-lift' patient transfer techniques; gives training in emergency evacuation; and educates people on back care and injury prevention. She educates and empowers people to identify and assess workplace ergonomic risks, as well as developing solutions.

Founder of Free to Be™ Rehab Consulting, Purdy was prompted to establish the company when she saw how hard it was for the general public to locate services and equipment to help with Musculo-Skeletal Injury (MSI) prevention, recovery and rehabilitation. When her mother was diagnosed with terminal cancer, Purdy found locating equipment difficult. A few years later, she started a retail/resource centre providing the tools for independence. This started her on a new venture that would change how she viewed her physiotherapy career—helping others help themselves. The retail store was eventually closed, but Purdy now assists families find solutions for themselves and their aging parents to keep them independent and mobile. She makes home assessments, provides professional assistance in choosing appropriate equipment, and gives PT/OT treatments. She helps them find solutions so they can get on with their life, moving from what they can't do to seeing what is possible. "I love being able to make a difference and contribute to others' well-being—to see a person take charge of their life and move beyond pain."

Her training programs include: Back in Control™; Get Me Out of Here!™ (emergency evacuation); No-Lift Moves and Transfers™; plus Office Ergonomics—What Your Mother Never Told You. Purdy also works part-time as the ergonomics and injury-prevention advisor for Providence Health Care in Vancouver.

3597 West 23rd Avenue | Vancouver, BC | V6S 1K4 | Tel: 604.739.7315
Cell: 604.790.1999 | Fax: 604.739.7803 | Email: barbpurdy@freetobe.ca | www.freetobe.ca

The Garbha Institute and The Garbha Foundation

Bonnie Thorne
Founder and Chair

"We all have a yearning to develop and share our innate gifts and to cement a sense of belonging in the world, to leave our unique soul print that reflects our work and our contribution."—Bonnie Thorne

Garbha is a Sanskrit word meaning 'matrix' or 'womb'. It reflects the desire of Bonnie Thorne, founder of the Garbha Institute, to create a metaphorical space where individuals can fully develop their potential—of mind, body and spirit. The Institute's mission is to provide programs and services that enhance individual and community living within the framework of holistic healthcare and education. Its fraternal organization, the Garbha Foundation, accepts donations, raises funds and seeks sponsors so that the Institute may advance its mandate.

The Garbha Institute achieves its mission in two ways: by providing educational opportunities and by working in partnership with community organizations. All Garbha events and initiatives bridge conventional and holistic modalities, emphasizing a multidimensional view of health and education that incorporates physical, mental, emotional and spiritual components. Their programs and collaborations have at their core a commitment to personal and spiritual growth for all individuals. The five programs of the Institute focus on arts and healing, children and spirituality, education, hospice and outreach.

Thorne believes in partnerships. By building collaborative relationships with like-minded community organizations, the Garbha Institute and its partners are able to reach deeply into communities, inviting individuals to discover and practice full connection with the self—mentally, physically and spiritually. In keeping with the generosity of heart and spirit of established sponsors and volunteers, the Garbha Foundation welcomes contributions of support or donations so that the Garbha Institute may continue and deepen its dedication to service for the betterment of personal and community life.

213 – 3495 Cambie Street | Vancouver, BC | V5Z 4R3 | Tel: 604.728.3975
Email: info@garbhainstitute.com | www.garbhainstitute.com | www.garbhafoundation.com

L-R: Ray Leung, Paul Parolin, Keri Caruk, Randal Ius

Happy Planet Foods

Natural and Organic Juicecrafters

The first thing people notice about Happy Planet is that everything they represent and do lives up to their name, and they are happy to confirm their positive intentions on every bottle and carton. Their mission statement, "to astonish your taste buds, nourish your body, unite you with the best sources of food and drink on this planet, and grow a progressive business from which happiness flows," is a refreshing foretaste of the superlative 'juicecraft' that this 'microjuicery' company has to offer. With small batches made often, every juice is bursting with freshness, taste and nutrition. Coupled with their active Community Program, which has donated over one million bottles of juice to help community organizations raise funds, the folks at Happy Planet are contributing generously to the world's flow of happiness.

Happy Planet strives to utilize the sweetest and tastiest organic and natural ingredients, processing only fully ripened fruit as close as possible to where it is grown. For instance, the company only uses organic bananas grown by the Borja family in Ecuador. "Our passion is deeply rooted in healthy and sustainable food and the just society it creates. We strive to be an example of doing well by doing good," says Randal Ius, vice-president of business development. Their products are free of allergens, do not contain preservatives, colouring, artificial sweeteners, or anything else you can't pronounce.

For Happy Planet, their core values of health, happiness, creativity, fun and environmental stewardship go hand in hand with community involvement. Through its Community Partners Program, it supports groups promoting social justice and environmental causes, as well as food security and the arts. "Businesses have a responsibility to nurture the communities that support them," says Ius, "and this is one way of saying thank you to those organizations that are making this a happier world."

203 – 950 Powell Street | Vancouver, BC | V6A 1H9 | **Tel:** 1.800.811.3213
Fax: 604.253.7544 | **Email:** happy@happyplanet.com | **www.happyplanet.com**

Healing Place Homeopathic Centre

Dr Peter Dobias, DVM, HMC
Doctor of Veterinary Medicine,
Homeopathic Master Clinician

Veterinarian Dr Peter Dobias practices holistic veterinary medicine and homeopathy. He grew up in Czechoslovakia, in a family with a long tradition of herbology, homeopathy and holistic healing. His grandfather was a herbologist and his father a veterinarian. After moving to Canada in 1991 and obtaining a Canadian veterinary license, Dr Dobias combined family traditions with the newest and most advanced forms of holistic veterinary care and homeopathy. "I could clearly see that the Western medical approach often has suppressive, but rarely true curative, effects," he says. "I observed that allopathic treatments often lead to other more serious problems, so I started looking at holistic treatment modalities." Consequently, he attended a few introductory courses in acupuncture and decided on homeopathy. The change, he says, was like learning to walk again, because the system of understanding the origins of disease is very different in homeopathy.

Dr Dobias and the Healing Place Homeopathic Centre's team understand that their animal friends are part of a family and that, if the animals are healthy, their owners feel better, too. The most rewarding part of their work is seeing a very sick patient recover with the use of homeopathy and energy healing when traditional Western methods have failed. "There is no doubt that holistic medicine and homeopathy provide the missing piece in our healthcare system," says Dr Dobias. "They are the key to health, balance and longevity for you and your animal friends."

The Centre's environment emphasizes natural materials, soothing colours and pleasant light and it features a comfortable examination couch (there are no metal examination tables in the clinic). Chemical disinfectants and cleaners have been replaced with natural products and an off-site surgical facility is used to reduce chemical smells. On top of that, the Centre's treat jar is never empty. It's no wonder their patients love return visits.

233 Seymour River Place | North Vancouver, BC | V7H 2N8 | Tel: 604.983.0987
Fax: 604.983.0985 | Email: healingplace@telus.net | www.healingplace.ca

L-R: Bayne Boyes, Lorna Hancock

Health Action Network Society

Lorna J. Hancock, Executive Director
Bayne E. Boyes, CMA, President

For Lorna Hancock, there is nothing more rewarding than being a port in a storm, a good listener, and offering clients key information so they can help themselves overcome a personal health crisis. Hancock is Executive Director of the Health Action Network Society (HANS). She believes in a special, integrated approach to healthcare, where information retrieval and personal choice are key elements of healing. HANS, founded in 1984, is a membership-based charity with a mandate to facilitate individual wellness through education and networking.

Sometimes someone may succumb to illness when a simple answer may have been right around the corner. In many cases, the critical difference in improved wellness comes not from a single modality, but from a combination of many therapies administered by an integrated team of practitioners. Of additional support to HANS members is the society's online health library (the largest in BC), which provides books, videos, audio tapes and references to support individuals on their personal health quest; a lending library is currently in the works. HANS keeps its membership current on health and environmental issues with a twice-monthly e-newsletter and a weekly news update on its website. HANS also hosts a number of educational events and forums and receives up to 25,000 enquiries a year from British Columbians.

HANS' President, Bayne Boyes, sees a higher purpose in the work of HANS. He and the entire team are passionate about providing information, choices, and options for all. "Science is only part of the solution to solving health problems. This big health club called HANS, which works on behalf of the individual, forges new ground in the dialogue surrounding healthcare. We hope to continue to make a difference for individual Canadians in the years to come."

202 – 5262 Rumble Street | Burnaby, BC | V5J 2B6 | Tel: 604.435.0512
Fax: 604.435.1561 | Email: lorna@hans.org | www.hans.org

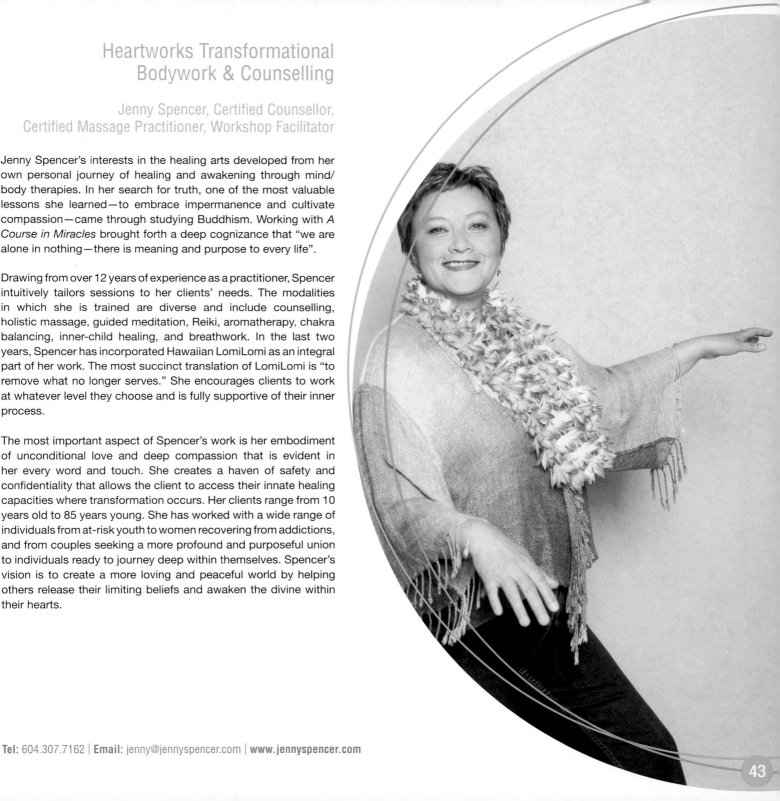

Heartworks Transformational Bodywork & Counselling

Jenny Spencer, Certified Counsellor, Certified Massage Practitioner, Workshop Facilitator

Jenny Spencer's interests in the healing arts developed from her own personal journey of healing and awakening through mind/body therapies. In her search for truth, one of the most valuable lessons she learned—to embrace impermanence and cultivate compassion—came through studying Buddhism. Working with *A Course in Miracles* brought forth a deep cognizance that "we are alone in nothing—there is meaning and purpose to every life".

Drawing from over 12 years of experience as a practitioner, Spencer intuitively tailors sessions to her clients' needs. The modalities in which she is trained are diverse and include counselling, holistic massage, guided meditation, Reiki, aromatherapy, chakra balancing, inner-child healing, and breathwork. In the last two years, Spencer has incorporated Hawaiian LomiLomi as an integral part of her work. The most succinct translation of LomiLomi is "to remove what no longer serves." She encourages clients to work at whatever level they choose and is fully supportive of their inner process.

The most important aspect of Spencer's work is her embodiment of unconditional love and deep compassion that is evident in her every word and touch. She creates a haven of safety and confidentiality that allows the client to access their innate healing capacities where transformation occurs. Her clients range from 10 years old to 85 years young. She has worked with a wide range of individuals from at-risk youth to women recovering from addictions, and from couples seeking a more profound and purposeful union to individuals ready to journey deep within themselves. Spencer's vision is to create a more loving and peaceful world by helping others release their limiting beliefs and awaken the divine within their hearts.

Tel: 604.307.7162 | **Email:** jenny@jennyspencer.com | **www.jennyspencer.com**

Hilary Mackey, BA, RCC

Body Psychotherapist

Through 20 years of training, self-exploration and experience as a body worker in private practice, Hilary Mackey has developed her own distinctive method, which she calls Awareness Body Psychotherapy. Her passionate, lifelong interest in the body/mind connection has led her to study a wide variety of therapeutic methodologies: touch, sound, movement, creativity and energy-centred therapies, meditation, and psychological methods including trauma repair. The integration of this rich experiential background is the foundation of her work as a Registered Clinical Counsellor. Her Body Psychotherapy brings to light the connection between physical and emotional discomfort. "The body is the language of the unconscious and stores a constant stream of messages," she says. "By becoming aware of the unconscious, we access the power of our own truth and can use it to make choices that will enhance our lives."

Awareness is central to Mackey's work. In a private session, she establishes a safe environment through respectful, focused touch and verbal work that allows clients to heal in an atmosphere of support and acceptance. With self-awareness, clients move forward at their own pace into ownership of buried feelings and beliefs. The results are relaxation, spontaneity and a greater sense of possibility in one's life. Mackey finds groups to be important for working with the shame and isolation of trauma, and has logged over 2000 hours as a leader, co-leader and participant. Several times a year she offers an experiential training workshop, The Body and Psychotherapy, to people who are professionally and personally interested in the topic.

"Hilary Mackey has an outstanding ability to combine courageous body therapy with safe and empathic counselling, which releases the injured person from the prison of the wounded self," says psychologist Dr Patricia Wilensky. In addition to her practice in Vancouver, Mackey has presented and worked internationally, and maintains a practice in Seattle, Washington for sessions and training.

Awareness Body Psychotherapy | 3026 Arbutus Street, 2nd Floor | Vancouver, BC | V6J 4P7 | **Tel:** 604.251.9057
Toll Free: 1.877.251.9057 | **Email:** hilary@bodypsychotherapy.ca | **www.bodypsychotherapy.ca**

44

Hollyhock Centre

Dana Bass Solomon, CEO, Board Member of PIVOT Foundation, Steering Committee Member of the Hollyhock Leadership Institute

Hollyhock Centre, a non-profit society, located in the natural splendour of Cortes Island, is Canada's leading educational retreat centre. Located 160km north of Vancouver, this 44-acre centre was founded to inspire, nourish and support people who are making the world better. In the early 80s, Hollyhock's founders dreamed of becoming stewards of the land and creating a place where they could live in community and build a sanctuary for reflection, healing and learning. Today, it is the perfect place to access world-class presenters exploring themes in the areas of wisdom and wellness, arts, culture, business, leadership and social change. The centre's goal is to increase the role of engaged citizenry, while offering rest, rejuvenation and holiday time.

In an atmosphere that supports learning, growing and just being, the Hollyhock experience is an alchemical mix of spectacular wilderness, cozy accommodations, gourmet organic meals, interesting people, morning yoga, exceptional bodywork, peace, quiet and a breathtaking garden.

"The beautiful garden at Hollyhock is a metaphor for the work we're doing here," says Dana Bass Solomon, CEO, "—preparing the soil, planting the seeds for positive social change, caring for our earth, and supporting people who are doing great work." Hollyhock is paradise with a purpose. The experience of being on the land, connecting in a deep and meaningful way with people of diverse cultures and similar values, can help individuals fulfill their potential and direct their energy towards positive change in their local communities. Solomon is dedicated to ensuring that people of all means can experience Hollyhock and she is a passionate fundraiser for the Hollyhock Scholarship Fund. "Scholarship support initiates a ripple effect of far-reaching change that touches the lives of individuals, their families and communities."

In addition to their annually published free catalogue, Hollyhock distributes a monthly e-newsletter featuring programs, urban events, garden tips, co-sponsorships, recipes and holiday specials.

PO Box 127 ML | Cortes Island, BC | V0P 1K0 | **Tel:** 1.800.933.6339
Email: registration@hollyhock.ca | **www.hollyhock.ca**

45

Hollyhock Leadership Institute

Karen Mahon
Executive Director

The Hollyhock Leadership Institute is a school for social change dedicated to empowering current and emerging leaders to create high-impact social transformation. The Institute helps individuals and groups develop skills, build alliances, catalyze new visions and rekindle inspiration. Its programs address a range of issues, from spiritual activism and women's leadership to fundraising and community organizing. Some programs are offered in tandem with the Institute's partner, the Hollyhock Centre on Cortes Island.

Made accessible to a wide range of people and organizations through subsidized rates, the Institute's programs have reached more than 2000 people across Canada and the US since it opened in 1997. Their programs build bridges across issues, cultural differences and geographical areas, as well as between grassroots, national and international organizations. One of the most important aspects of the Institute's work is creating community— by convening strategy sessions to increase collaboration and effectiveness among people and organizations working towards common goals. The connections between different communities and perspectives create new synergies, ideas and projects that exponentially increase the impact of their individual efforts. At the same time, these connections further the development of a stronger, more just and sustainable society.

"If there is anywhere on earth that society can make the U-turn towards sustainability, it is here," says the Institute's Executive Director Karen Mahon, well known for her environmental work with Greenpeace and other advocacy organizations. "With its independent thinkers and some of the highest levels of economic well-being, intact natural systems and environmental values anywhere in the world, BC has all the ingredients for meeting the challenges of the 21st century. We know that social movements triumph through skilled, strategic and inspired leadership. The Hollyhock Institute is dedicated to forging the leaders of the future."

680 – 220 Cambie Street | Vancouver, BC | V6B 2M9 | Tel: 604.669.4802 | Fax: 604.647.6612
Cell: 604.936.5992 | Email: karen@hollyhockleadership.org | www.hollyhockleadership.org

Huemanbeing

Madeleine Bachan Kaur
Kundalini Yoga Teacher, Artist, Musician,
Leader of Aquarian Consciousness

Kundalini Yoga Teacher, Madeleine Bachan Kaur is dedicated to the service of higher consciousness and uses her gifts as a teacher, artist and musician to inspire others to see themselves clearly, love themselves deeply, be themselves fearlessly and liberate the world through their radiance. Kundalini Yoga (as taught by Yogi Bhajan) is a technology of awareness that allows us to experience and explore our true identity and potential as human beings. Physically, it strengthens and promotes health of the body's systems; mentally, it clears and balances the mind; spiritually, it awakens the awareness of our true nature developing a relationship with the radiance of soul. "Through Kundalini yoga and my own acceptance of God Consciousness, it became clear to me that yoga, art and music are my divine path," says Bachan Kaur.

Her enlightening services include lessons in being open and in listening more intently to the Divine within each of us. She helps those she touches to recognize the truth within themselves and to have the courage to follow that truth, to live the experience of destiny. "The Guru, the great teacher that delivers us from ignorance to enlightenment is alive in every breath, every moment, every situation and every being," says Bachan Kaur. "It is my prayer that we learn more deeply every day to recognize the Guru within us and our lives so that our humility can be vast enough to allow God to breathe deeply through us."

Bachan Kaur inspires others through her sacred-music CDs, visual art and creative visionary thinking. She believes that true healing is beyond the ego and comes from surrender to the radiance of the Infinite within. "In daily life, it is important to meditate, smile to all, and remember the other person is you."

Tel: 604.773.0857 | Email: bachan@huemanbeing.com | www.huemanbeing.com

Ilona Hedi Granik

Clairvoyant, Author,
Spiritual Health Coach

At times, everyone needs healing—a psychic tune-up—and Ilona Granik, as a clairaudience, clairvoyance and telepathy expert, can help one achieve this. Born into a family of actors, she had an unconventional childhood surrounded by astrologers and artists. She started working professionally as a psychic medium in 1992 and has a very special way of sharing her gifts with clients. "Sitting quietly, I tune into a client's unique vibration. Then, relative to the area of emotion that I see, feel and hear hovering over them and around their auric field and energy body, I ask questions, gently coaxing issues to rise up for emotional release," explains Granik. "In most sessions, people have a deep emotional breakthrough and illumination." In her practice, Granik also uses a Quantum biofeedback device that transmits 65 million tiny electromagnetic signals into the body each second, providing valuable biofeedback to her clients. Its sophisticated technology picks up the earliest signs of imbalance or stress.

Granik has been featured on television and in newspapers, and has facilitated healing workshops and dynamic conference presentations. She writes two astrology columns for Canadian publications and has written and produced two spoken-word CDs. The first, *Chakras: Pathways to Well-Being*, is an educational CD; the second, *Inner Being: Meditations Within the Elemental Kingdoms*, is a fully guided meditation that focuses on each chakra. "This CD helps you become aware of the elemental kingdoms through music and tonal keys that guide you, grounding your consciousness in present time," she says of *Inner Being*.

As a gifted healer dedicated to helping others, Granik's wish is that "more people could fall freely into the arms of grace and have the chance to know God and the Goddess intimately. I wish all people could live their dreams and be powerful enough to know and heal themselves."

Email: iamilona@gmail.com | www.heartlightcentre.com

InHouseSpa™ Corporation

Timothy Bullinger
Founder

The first spas were developed by ancient Roman, Greek, Egyptian, Mesopotamian and Minoan cultures for social bathing, healing and to treat aches and wounds. They referred to these spas as 'health by water' or 'Solus Per Aqua' hence the acronym 'spa'. Later in history, other cultures integrated spas into their traditions in a variety of ways, always keeping true to the original purpose of 'health by water'. Timothy Bullinger, a leading international architect/designer, has 20 years of experience conceiving and creating custom estates, residences and resort spas. "I blend designs based on ancient cultures and traditions with modern technologies that are conscious, considerate and respectful of our environment," he says.

His company, InHouseSpa™ creates exclusive in-home natural spas where one can experience mental, physical and spiritual well-being in a relaxing, spiritual and calming environment. Bullinger offers clients the opportunity to create and enjoy the spa experience in their own home 'wellness centre'. From a simple meditation or massage area to a full-facility spa, incorporating pools, hydrotherapy, steam, aromatherapy, multi-spray showers, massage, esthetics and body treatments, the possibilities for an in-house spa are endless. InHouseSpa incorporates natural and organic building materials and green energy sources, such as geothermal, solar and wind technologies that produce electricity, heating and cooling, whenever possible.

Bullinger's designs reflect the historic traditions of spas: "I integrate ancient design principles and methodologies such as feng shui, wabi sabi, vedic and native, which relate to energy, harmony and aesthetics." Following these principles, the spas attract positive life energy, or chi (in the case of feng shui), so that energy flows smoothly in the space. InHouseSpa is involved in every step of the process, from design through to the arranging and overseeing of the spa's construction, then educating the owner on the use of the spa and its equipment upon its completion.

237 – 1628 West 1st Avenue | Vancouver, BC | V6J 1G1 | Tel: 1.877.Spa.Now2
Fax: 604.739.7914 | Email: spa@inhousespa.com | www.inhousespa.com

Integral City Systems

Marilyn Hamilton, PhD, CGA
Integral City Meshworker, Writer,
Facilitator, Researcher, Professor

A dynamic and multi-faceted facilitator for urban change, Dr Marilyn Hamilton promotes global intelligences in leaders, teams, organizations, sectors, communities and cities. As the founder of Integral City, she envisions cities as the resilient, vibrant habitat of humanity—just as vibrant and optimized for humans as a beehive is for bees. And just as bees pollinate their life conditions for positive, co-creative sustainability, her Integral City systems are designed to generate optimal conditions that add value to the evolution of the planet. Blending frameworks and technologies from integral, spiral dynamics and living system approaches, Hamilton 'meshworks' or interweaves people, purpose, priorities, profits, programs and processes to bring about change that is ecologically informed and operationally integrated. Hamilton facilitates enquiries, assessments, capacity-building practices and collaboration through her vast network of interdisciplinary connections in the community, workplace, Royal Roads University, The Banff Centre and Adizes Graduate School.

"Enabling the release of human capacity in a coherent way, by designing a 'meshwork' that allows everyone and everything to flex and flow, is the most rewarding aspect of my work," says Hamilton. "When people become intentional and commit to working together to bring about change, I see the magnificence of human potential evolving."

As the author of well-being, learning and leadership assessments, several books on leadership and wellness, and a discovery learning game, Hamilton has a strong voice that connects networks from around the world, catalyzing their power, authority and influence for global well-being. Her Maple Leaf Memes project—a mapping of Canada's values systems—is just one of her numerous initiatives to promote greater human emergence and global health. Presenting a world of possibilities, and an education in itself, her website offers services, products, training and intelligence for the global village—helping BC to steward its resources in sustainable and ecologically friendly ways.

24 – 4001 Old Clayburn Road | Abbotsford, BC | V3G 1C5 | **Tel:** 604.855.8478
Cell: 604.614.1822 | **Fax:** 604.855.8870 | **Email:** marilyn@integralcity.com | **www.integralcity.com**

International Centre for Sustainable Cities

Action on Urban Sustainability

Founded in 1993 as an alliance between governments, the private sector and civil society organizations, the International Centre for Sustainable Cities (ICSC) is a formidable force embracing the hearts and souls of cities worldwide. ICSC is a catalyst, bringing lessons from Canada and around the globe to show how urban sustainability can be implemented. "We are a 'do-tank' not a 'think-tank'," says ICSC president and CEO Dr Nola-Kate Seymoar.

With an impressive track record of helping cities resolve problems relating to urban growth, ICSC takes a participatory approach to creating sustainable urban futures. The centre works with partners from all sectors to enhance the environmental, social, cultural and economic well-being of cities and communities. It hosts a network of cities looking out 50 to 100 years to develop long-term visions, medium-term strategies and immediate actions that will set a course for livable and resilient communities. "Sustainability is about the future—the quality of life that will be possible for our grandchildren," says Dr Seymoar. She encourages people to get engaged by understanding how our actions today—including conserving energy, working towards solving global warming, supporting responsible businesses, eating local produce, using public transportation and much more—will have a long-term impact globally.

ICSC was one of the partners in Cities PLUS, the award-winning 100-year vision for sustainability in Greater Vancouver. The centre has also founded a series of breakfast meetings designed to strengthen relationships with like-minded organizations and individuals in the Lower Mainland. "Vancouver is a hotbed of ideas, expertise and technologies on urban sustainability," says Seymoar. "We want to have ICSC and Greater Vancouver recognized internationally as leaders in this field."

415 – 1788 West 5th Avenue | Vancouver, BC | V6J 1P2 | **Tel:** 604.666.0061
Fax: 604.666.0009 | **Email:** info@icsc.ca | **www.icsc.ca** | **www.plusnetwork.org**

Clockwise L-R: Dominica Babicki, Paul Evans, Jane McRae, Samantha Anderson, Denise Pritchard, John Calimente Susana Tapia, Nola-Kate Seymoar, Natalia Verand, Ewa Izdebski, Absent: Sumana Wijerathne, Wendy Holm, Y.R. Radhika, Lama Mugabo, Isabel Budke, Zoe Mullard

Jan Mills

Inspirational Speaker,
Health and Wellness Coach

With an extensive background in international event marketing, public relations and television production, Jan Mills has inspired, motivated and empowered individuals and companies throughout Canada and the US. Nominated for an Ethics in Action Award in 1999, Mills has applied her facilitation skills and motivational speeches to strategic partnership building and corporate social responsibility, as well as triumph over adversity, disease prevention and balanced living.

Diagnosed with multiple sclerosis in 1986, Mills developed many of her strengths as a result of personal adversity. For 11 years, she suffered bouts of paralysis and blindness, yet continued to head her successful company. It was only when car accidents exacerbated her condition—spurring her to research and implement a targeted nutritional supplement regime—that she regained her health and experienced newfound gratitude for things she had previously taken for granted. "It's amazing how beautiful the sunset is when you've lost your eyesight for a week or how enjoyable a walk on a beach is when you've been in a wheelchair for a month," says Mills. With humour and gratitude, she has learned to look for silver linings—such as seeing her temporary leg numbness, due to MS, as an ideal time for leg waxing!

"I am blessed with the opportunity to utilize my research and life challenges to inspire others to embrace change, take responsibility for their own health, make informed choices about wellness options and ignite hope for overcoming personal or business challenges," she says.

Former president of Canadian Business for Social Responsibility, Mills demonstrates integrity, excellence and lightheartedness in all that she does. Her speeches and writings inspire and educate with humour and insight while her health and wellness expertise provide holistic direction for achieving optimal well-being. A dynamic leader, Mills provides an example of best practice for others to emulate.

3948 Gallagher's Parkway | Kelowna, BC | V1W 3Z8
Tel: 250.979.0008 | Email: jan@janmills.net | www.janmills.net

John's Acupuncture Clinic

John Blazevic, RAc, BSc
Clinical Director

John William Blazevic is an acupuncturist, doctor of Traditional Chinese Medicine, president of the Traditional Chinese Medicine Association of BC and a professor at South Bay College of Traditional Oriental Medicine. His teachers, Edward Obaidey Sensei, Ikeda Masakazu Sensei and Sam Tam Sifu, inspired and shaped his career. These three enlightened beings showed him how wonderful life is once you realize universal life energy does exist. Blazevic's belief in the power of chi or life energy is paramount in his work. In acupuncture, thin needles are inserted into specific points on the energetic pathways (meridians and collaterals) to restore a patient's balance. According to ancient theories, disease is thought to occur when the body's balance is disrupted due to the poor flow of three elements: energy, blood and fluids.

Blazevic follows the classical theories of Chinese Medicine, promoting what is natural and not using force in treatment or life. "I treat the individual, not the disease." At John's Acupuncture Clinic, the focus is on helping individuals become healthy and recover from illness by using traditional principles for vitality, health and longevity. "It is vital that people learn how to live healthy lives," he says. Along with acupuncture, the clinic employs many ancient moxibustion techniques not commonly used. Moxibustion is the burning of the herb mugwort on the body to improve circulation and strengthen the blood.

Blazevic treats each individual based on his or her unique flow of chi. He says that if the patient is weak, then gentle, nurturing (tonifying) treatment is performed. If the patient has a blockage, a shunting or drainage treatment is performed to remove the blockage. "Seeing patients recover from illness, helping them understand that they have the innate ability to do so, and studying and employing the theories of Traditional Chinese Medicine are the most rewarding aspects of my work."

4347 West 10th Avenue | Vancouver, BC | V6R 2H6 | **Tel:** 604.224.6692
Email: john@johnsacupuncture.com | **www.johnsacupuncture.com**

Julia King

Energy Healer, Channel, Spiritual Teacher, Co-founder of the Live Peace Foundation, Angel Therapy Practitioner®, certified by Doreen Virtue, PhD

An intuitive healer and spiritual teacher, Julia King helps individuals, couples and families tap into their personal power and heal body, mind and spirit. By intuitively scanning the body and interpreting the energy field of her clients, she provides valuable insights and information about their unconscious behavioural patterns, past lives, relationship issues and overall health.

King is also dedicated to healing at the global level. "There comes a time in life when you stop and ask yourself what you can do to make this world a better place," she says. As co-founder of the Live Peace Foundation, her personal contribution comes in the form of engaging others in small changes that will collectively improve the Earth and bring more peace and harmony into our everyday lives. Based on the belief that synchronized intention for peace can create a new reality, King teaches others to focus their powerful energy on creating that positive intention.

The Foundation is an educational organization that promotes these concepts with retreats and workshops for schools, businesses, community groups and individuals. It teaches tools of empowerment, such as the one-minute World Peace Wave Meditation (a synchronized meditation to be done at noon in all time zones worldwide), dynamic visualization and cognitive restructuring. King is as passionate about her work as she is about being part of a greater community for change. "I feel exhilarated when I can be an agent of healing and growth in someone's life," she says. "Each person is a living powerhouse of potential and, when that power is activated in a positive way, it can have a huge impact on the planet." For clients outside of BC, King offers phone consultations, distance healings and in-home sessions, helping people of all ages and stages in life to find the answers they need to live powerfully.

4624 West 15th Avenue | Vancouver, BC | V6R 3B6 | Tel: 604.731.5479
Email: powerofyes@hotmail.com | www.diamonddivinityhealing.com | www.worldpeacewave.com

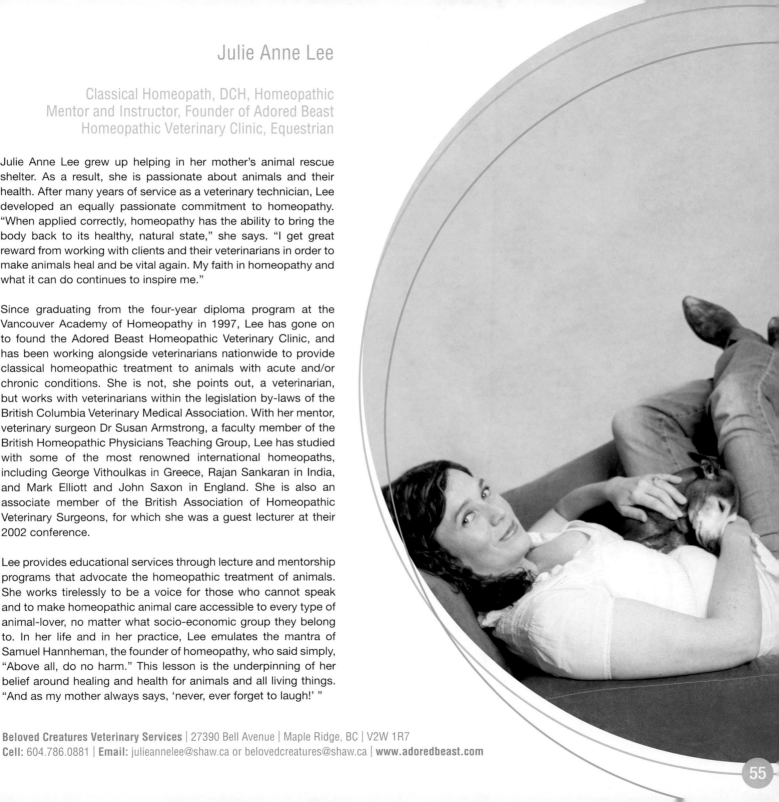

Julie Anne Lee

Classical Homeopath, DCH, Homeopathic
Mentor and Instructor, Founder of Adored Beast
Homeopathic Veterinary Clinic, Equestrian

Julie Anne Lee grew up helping in her mother's animal rescue shelter. As a result, she is passionate about animals and their health. After many years of service as a veterinary technician, Lee developed an equally passionate commitment to homeopathy. "When applied correctly, homeopathy has the ability to bring the body back to its healthy, natural state," she says. "I get great reward from working with clients and their veterinarians in order to make animals heal and be vital again. My faith in homeopathy and what it can do continues to inspire me."

Since graduating from the four-year diploma program at the Vancouver Academy of Homeopathy in 1997, Lee has gone on to found the Adored Beast Homeopathic Veterinary Clinic, and has been working alongside veterinarians nationwide to provide classical homeopathic treatment to animals with acute and/or chronic conditions. She is not, she points out, a veterinarian, but works with veterinarians within the legislation by-laws of the British Columbia Veterinary Medical Association. With her mentor, veterinary surgeon Dr Susan Armstrong, a faculty member of the British Homeopathic Physicians Teaching Group, Lee has studied with some of the most renowned international homeopaths, including George Vithoulkas in Greece, Rajan Sankaran in India, and Mark Elliott and John Saxon in England. She is also an associate member of the British Association of Homeopathic Veterinary Surgeons, for which she was a guest lecturer at their 2002 conference.

Lee provides educational services through lecture and mentorship programs that advocate the homeopathic treatment of animals. She works tirelessly to be a voice for those who cannot speak and to make homeopathic animal care accessible to every type of animal-lover, no matter what socio-economic group they belong to. In her life and in her practice, Lee emulates the mantra of Samuel Hannheman, the founder of homeopathy, who said simply, "Above all, do no harm." This lesson is the underpinning of her belief around healing and health for animals and all living things. "And as my mother always says, 'never, ever forget to laugh!' "

Beloved Creatures Veterinary Services | 27390 Bell Avenue | Maple Ridge, BC | V2W 1R7
Cell: 604.786.0881 | **Email:** julieannelee@shaw.ca or belovedcreatures@shaw.ca | **www.adoredbeast.com**

Karen Popoff

Transformationalist

Karen Popoff learned very early in life that she was a gifted intuitive. "As a child, I spent a great deal of time learning how my gifts worked and how to best use them for helping myself and others," she says. She trained with a mentor and continues to develop and enhance her gifts through regular meditation and journaling. "I find that I can hear the voices of Source, my guides and other great helpers of power in total clarity through both of these methods of communion and connection," says Popoff. "When they speak, the language is often very ancient and full of great truth, creating a calming force within me." She now shares her wisdom by teaching metaphysical principles to others. "I teach my students how to access their power without rituals and often recommend these methods to my clients."

Popoff acts as a gentle, yet highly effective, catalyst for change in individuals. She helps clients identify and understand what is blocking them, and why. She works on five levels—energetic, emotional, mental, physical and spiritual—to help her clients transform their lives and achieve their full potential. "I show the person how to transcend the barriers that are preventing them from moving forward in their lives, allowing for a shift in paradigm—sometimes in as little as a one-hour session," she says. "When we begin to see things differently," she explains, "it shifts our mindset or thought patterns, allowing us to open to new possibilities, and it is then that transformation can occur." The result is a deep awareness of truth that brings positive change on all levels. Her clients often describe their progress as awe-inspiring and testify to a renewed sense of hope and empowerment. "As I do this work that I was born to do, and as I move further into the full potential of myself, I feel a great sense of joy knowing that I am helping people move closer to fulfilling their full potential," says Popoff.

Tel: 604.688.0010 | **Email:** thetransformationalist@msn.com
www.thetransformationalist.com | www.karenpopoff.com

Katyanna Gabriel

Spiritual Counsellor, Healer, Clairvoyant

"I believe spirituality and healing are lifelong journeys," says spiritual counsellor and healer Katyanna Gabriel. "My ability as a medium between the physical plane and the spirit world allows me to provide accurate predictions in life, love, career, relationships, business and community development, as well as legal matters." In her practice, she utilizes a diverse set of skills: she is a Registered Reflexologist, Reiki Master, aromatherapist, yoga instructor and doula/birth assistant; she also reads Tarot and oracles.

Gabriel helps families and individuals to release and cleanse spirits that have died in trauma and shock. She also helps remove negative energy residue from past conflicts or trauma. Gabriel not only provides guidance and healing from past and present emotional traumas and injury, she also provides counselling, mediation and conflict resolution services to individuals, couples and groups. A unique aspect of her work is her dedication to training individuals in psychic development and the healing arts. Through the use of ritual and ceremony, she creates an environment where the individual is open and able to unlock his or her spiritual and healing gifts. As well, she offers clients readings from The Elemental Oracle—a spiritual and ecological Tarot deck of her own design that provides insight and predictions regarding her clients, their relationships and their environment. The Oracle honours the sacredness, wisdom and knowledge held in the wild places of the earth.

Gabriel believes that the adversity we experience in our lifetimes can become a powerful tool for change. She supports the healing process of her clients by quickly assessing the individual's needs and providing the appropriate healing methodology. A gifted intuitive, Gabriel assists clients in resolving significant life issues. "I offer a straightforward, honest and respectful approach to all who engage my services," she says, "and I provide an authentic connection through my unique gifts to your spirit and your spirit guides."

Tel: 778.838.6517 | Email: info@katyannagabriel.com | www.katyannagabriel.com

Kids Around the World
Children's Museum Society

Jessie Smith
Founder and Executive Director, Children's Educator

Kids Around the World Children's Museum Society's goal is to create a permanent children's museum to encourage intercultural understanding, foster a sense of global citizenship, and promote sustainability. While working towards this goal, the Society is taking its exhibits on tour and seeking community support.

Kids Around the World produces enchanting 'must-touch' exhibits and engaging programs that teach visitors about the lives of kids around the world and help visitors understand the diverse cultures of Greater Vancouver. The Society's exhibits and programs create a learning environment that incorporates the very best of early childhood education practices. The Museum creates experiences that reinforce a child's fertile sense of wonder, creativity, curiosity and imagination. The exhibits and programs strengthen motor skills, problem solving, communication, and language skills—key areas of childhood development. The exhibit *Tigers and Dragons: China and India for Kids* visited Granville Island and Gastown on its tour of Vancouver's Lower Mainland. "Our hope is that when children get to know their 'neighbours' in Vancouver and around the world, they will be inspired to be lifelong engaged citizens, and will want to help solve the problems facing the city, the nation and the planet," says Jessie Smith, founder and executive director of the Society.

There are more than 200 children's museums giving children a voice in the United States, but there are only five in Canada. Kids Around the World wants to give children the chance to experience the wonder of the world without having to step on a plane. To do that, the Society welcomes the public's interest and assistance through visiting an exhibit, volunteering, or donating towards a permanent museum. Information on current exhibit locations is listed at www.kidsaroundtheworld.ca.

PO Box 21595, Little Italy Postal Outlet | 1424 Commercial Drive | Vancouver, BC | V5L 5G2
Tel: 604.708.2298 | **Email:** jessie@kidsaroundtheworld.ca | **www.kidsaroundtheworld.ca**

Kira Frketich, ND

Naturopathic Doctor, Public Educator, Speaker

Dr Kira Frketich, affectionately known as Dr Kira to her patients, offers a broad range of therapies to her clients: acupuncture, homeopathy, nutrition, herbal medicine, Bowen Therapy™, and Emotional Freedom Technique ™ (EFT). She specializes in therapeutic diet work, digestive disorders, food sensitivities and detoxification. She also has considerable experience dealing with women's health issues and the treatment of children, allergies, eczema, depression and anxiety, and autoimmune disorders. Dr Kira happily offers phone consultations and arranges teleconferences and public speaking engagements across the country.

Dr Kira's knowledge and experience with a healthy diet began with her mother's motto: "I eat to live, not live to eat!" "My mother had us eating tofu, carob and brewer's yeast from the time we were young," says Dr Kira. "She was always going for the healthiest option she could find." Dr Kira's treatments are as much about education as they are about therapy. A treatment is a 'fix,' but the education that comes with the treatment can bring about a permanent change that leads to a lifetime of health. "I love to get people to the point where they understand their bodies and its needs, which instills them with the confidence to take an active role in their health," says Dr Kira.

Dr Kira is an eloquent advocate of healthy eating. She promotes whole, organic, local foods for optimal health and mood, and to keep you effective in your work, play and passion. She loves to offer clients recipes such as Spelt Porridge (2:1 water; spelt flakes with a pinch of Celtic sea salt, pumpkin seeds, pecans; add ground flax and blueberries at the end), or Spinach Stir-fry (sauté onions and mushrooms—use a variety of shitake, Portobello and brown mushrooms for extra flavour—until soft; add one bunch of spinach, salt and pepper to taste; cook until the spinach softens).

Life is Now

Neil Pearson, MSc, BScPT, BA-BPHE
Physiotherapist, Certified Yoga Therapist

Neil Pearson is a physiotherapist and yoga therapist specializing in pain management. This combination of therapies allows him to consider both the connections between, and the enormous adaptability of, the musculoskeletal tissues, the nervous system, breathing and the body-mind connection. His treatments offer the benefits of hands-on therapy, self-management and awareness exercises such as yoga. "The most rewarding thing about my work is hearing a client tell me that they have figured out what they need to do to decrease their pain, recover and grow," says Pearson.

He is passionate about supporting individual clients and teaching them the power of our nervous system to decrease pain and recover function. "Our nervous system will learn to do whatever we continue to teach it," he says. "Whenever we take positive actions with how we move our body, how we hold our posture, what we think and how we feel, we are making changes towards recovering abilities and decreasing pain." Pearson has developed Understand Pain; Recover Function seminars that teach people with chronic pain how the pain alarm system works and how they can reset their system and body so that they experience less pain. Besides instructing his clients, he also teaches healthcare professionals and yoga teachers about pain management, and he is developing therapeutic yoga classes for people with chronic pain.

"To deal with my own stress, I may turn to yoga, I may go for a long run on mountain trails, or I may let my soul and heart be carried away by listening to music," he says. "But the best de-stressor is the sound of my sons and wife laughing."

303 Cardiff Way | Port Moody, BC | V3H 3W4
Tel: 604.506.1195 | Email: neil@lifeisnow.ca | www.lifeisnow.ca

Living Oceans Society

Jennifer Lash
Executive Director

When Jennifer Lash established Living Oceans Society in 1998, she dreamed of changing the way our ocean is managed, thereby ensuring healthy waters, marine life and coastal communities for generations to come. Through education, advocacy, scientific research and policy development, her non-profit organization is making her dream a reality. Combining scientific analysis with local knowledge, Living Oceans Society exerts a positive force in marine conservation on Canada's Pacific Coast.

The Society is working towards closed containment salmon farming to protect wild salmon stocks, a coast permanently free of oil rigs and tanker traffic, a network of marine protected areas, and the adoption of sustainable fishing plans that prohibit over-fishing and protect habitats. Doing so requires challenging people to embrace new ideas that will ultimately benefit everyone. "People are part of the environment," says Lash, "and we must figure out how to live and work on the coast, while ensuring conservation of marine biological diversity. By protecting the ocean and promoting the right economic development, we help all forms of life to prosper."

In order to change the way the ocean is managed, the Society is helping to change people's perception of the ocean. Living Oceans Society runs campaigns that educate Canadians about the ocean's importance as a source of food and as an integral part of the global ecosystem. It also works with all levels of government to promote policy reform, and with coastal residents to ensure healthy communities. As a Living Oceans Society member, individuals can nurture this vision by choosing only sustainable seafood through the SeaChoice program, participating in online advocacy on their web page, sharing local knowledge about the marine environment, and educating decision-makers and the public on the threats to our marine environment.

235 First Street, Box 320 | Sointula, BC | V0N 3E0 | **Tel:** 250.973.6580
Fax: 250.973.6581 | **Email:** jenlash@livingoceans.org | **www.livingoceans.org**

LOHAS By Design

Zsoka Scurtescu
Founder and Lead Designer,
Co-founder of organics.bc.ca, Teacher

LOHAS stands for 'Lifestyles of Health and Sustainability'. The studio designs websites and provides printed marketing material that both advertises and promotes the lifestyle for which the company is eponymously named. "We support businesses that provide goods and services to the LOHAS market, appealing to consumers who value health, the environment, social justice, personal development and sustainable living," says Zsoka Scurtescu, founder and lead designer of LOHAS by Design.

Her company works with clients to develop corporate identities and messaging that revolve around health and sustainability. Scurtescu has come to realize that through her business she can help to lead her community in social responsibility. "Our vision is to help people see socially responsible and healthy choices so they can make our world a more just and sustainable place." Both a consumer and provider of LOHAS products and services herself, she understands her clients' target market, and this helps to provide a deep and meaningful connection with clients.

Originally from the corporate world, Scurtescu brings both a practical and a spiritual element to her work. "As my clients and I work together to create their 'look,' I love that we create something bigger than both of us. Sometimes we begin with nothing except the basic product or service and, through creating the brand, I see my clients become very proud of what they do. This gives both of us a great sense of achievement and adds another LOHAS provider to the marketplace."

In addition to providing web and graphic design services, Scurtescu also teaches web project management and programming one day a week at the Institute of Advanced Media in Vancouver. "I love to have the opportunity to pass on my knowledge and see my students become my colleagues." Another personal mission of hers is to educate the public about the organics movement, through her website, organics.bc.ca.

405 – 1641 Lonsdale Avenue | North Vancouver, BC | V7M 2J5
Tel: 604.762.1520 | Email: zsoka@lohasbydesign.ca | lohasbydesign.ca

Lunapads International Products Ltd

Madeleine Shaw and Suzanne Siemens
Co-founders

A dynamic duo from Vancouver are embracing their femininity and reconnecting women to the power and sacredness of their cycles in the 21st century. Madeleine Shaw and Suzanne Siemens are the owners of Lunapads International, a company that manufactures and markets natural feminine hygiene products, such as Lunapads washable pads and panty liners; Lunapanties padded underwear; the DivaCup, a menstrual cup; and natural sea sponge tampons. "Our products are definitely more environmentally responsible than disposable pads and tampons," says Shaw. "Using natural menstrual products actually helps women be more connected to, and more knowledgeable about, their bodies."

In 1999, Shaw and Siemens discovered that they shared a vision for better health for women and the planet. They combined their skills and mission to launch Lunapads with the purpose of creating "a more positive and informed relationship between women, their bodies and the earth." Today, Lunapads are used by thousands of women all over the world. Shaw and Siemens celebrate their success as business partners who educate, support and empower women. "We love that we have created a business that supports us, our families and the women who work with us," says Siemens. "It's a very positive and energized environment." At Lunapads, there's a real feeling of mutual trust and respect in every interaction with customers. The two women are proud to offer products with that kind of integrity and deep value. "Stirring up women's empowerment is a beautiful thing!" they say.

Lunapads products are available in many parts of the world including South Korea, Japan, Italy, France, Belgium and the UK, as well as in Canada and the US. Orders from the Lunapads website are shipped worldwide on a daily basis.

L-R: Suzanne Siemens, Madeleine Shaw

PO Box 3936 | Vancouver, BC | V6B 3Z4 | **Tel:** 604.681.9953 or 1.888.590.2299
Fax: 604.681.9904 | **Email:** info@lunapads.com | **www.lunapads.com**

Lynn McGown

Vocal/Singing Coach, Workshop Facilitator, Natural Voice Practitioner

With contagious passion and a lighthearted spirit, Lynn McGown has helped hundreds of individuals find and express the most profound level of their being through their voice. A singing/vocal coach and natural voice practitioner, she believes that everyone can sing and that exploring one's voice can create powerful life shifts. "Voice work is a portal to self-empowerment, healing and balance in body, mind and spirit," she says. "It can free you from anxiety and fears, while enhancing self-esteem."

McGown has been singing professionally for 25 years and has performed and led vocal workshops at international festivals, in concerts, for schools and at social and environmental benefits. She has sung and been interviewed live on CBC Radio and Radio Canada, among others, and trained with some of the world's best vocal teachers. As an Neuro-Linguistic Programming practitioner and life coach, she brings an intuitive dimension to her work, helping individuals to release emotional blocks and creating a safe space for them to sing their hearts out.

"It takes courage to discover your unique voice," says McGown. "Many people feel they can't sing because they've been criticized in the past, so doing vocal work often involves facing fears and freeing oneself from negative internal dialogues." But, she says, "taking risks and exploring one's full voice range has many positive ripple effects—boosting energy levels, balancing the nervous system, enhancing self-confidence and emotional well-being, decreasing stress and fatigue, and promoting fuller self-expression and creativity."

Offering workshops, tele-classes, private coaching and seminars, as well as concerts at her music retail store, Celtic Traditions, McGown is also the co-founder of the Jericho Folk Club—an annual showcase for accomplished local musicians, which fosters a vibrant musical community. "A community that sings together breathes together as one," says McGown. "Our voice is just waiting for our heart to open and our imagination to take flight."

1838 Balaclava Street | Vancouver, BC | V6K 4B8 | **Tel:** 604.222.4113 or 604.222.2299
Email: lynnmcgown@shaw.ca | **www.lynnmcgown.com** | **www.celtictraditions.ca**

Mahara Brenna

Holistic Rebirther, Mediator, Spiritual Counsellor,
International Facilitator, Speaker

The healing power of the land has greatly influenced Mahara Brenna's life and work. Born in Vancouver, Brenna has often quoted the First Nations people's declaration of Vancouver as the "City of the Sacred Marriage" in recognition of the joining of the mountains with the ocean—the unity and natural balance of the male and female. As an emissary of the divine feminine, a mediator and a community builder, Brenna has dedicated her life to restoring that balance in the individual, in couples and on a planetary scale.

"My work as a holistic rebirther assists people in healing emotionally and spiritually. By employing connected breathing in conjunction with 'Psychology of Vision' reprogramming, one releases the wounds of the past, frees the body to begin its healing, and liberates the inner light of the soul." Brenna's own metamorphosis began her career as a healer. For the first half of her life, she suffered from epilepsy and constant seizures. She was told it was incurable and she would live a severely restricted life. It was through the work she now shares with others that she healed the epilepsy. What was the greatest gift epilepsy taught her? "Death, leaving here, is the easy part...being fully present and 100% engaged with life now—that's the challenge. But oh, what a remarkable journey it is!"

As a mediator, Brenna has a passion for helping people to communicate more effectively, to listen and honour each other's differences and to discover the creativity and emotional satisfaction in resolving conflict. As a community builder and performer, she has facilitated groups as large as 7,000 in weaving experiences of harmony that celebrate our diverse 'family of humankind' and the seasons and cycles of mother earth. Brenna is proud of the strides her community has taken in the integration of alternative healing. When she began as a practitioner in 1977, holistic health and spiritual healing were seen as the far edge of fringe. "During the past 30 years, Vancouver has become the Canadian Mecca for healing. Now people flock here for both personal transformation and professional training in the healing arts, natural medicines, spiritual development and new thought therapies ...to the 'City of the Sacred Marriage'. "

1690 West 63rd Avenue | Vancouver, BC | V6P 2H8 | **Tel:** 604.221.0787 | **Cell:** 604.802.6274
Fax: 604.221.5454 | **Email:** maharabrenna@telus.net | **www.maharabrenna.com**

Mama Goddess Birth Shop

Nikiah Seeds
Owner, Certified Birthing From Within Mentor,
Circle Leader

Nikiah Seeds holds a wise mantra close to her heart: "If you do what you love for a living, you will never work a day in your life!" She is the spirited owner of both Mama Goddess Birth Shop—an online store for birthing families and a source of supplies for doulas and midwives—and the Seeds of Birth education centre, which offers 'Birthing from Within' prenatal classes.

Seeds applies her wisdom and passion to help parents and parents-to-be. A former birth doula, she brings her love of herbs along with her skills as a reflexologist and parent into the birthing room, classroom and business. "It is my goal to provide pregnant women and their partners with all the information they need to make informed and empowered choices around the birth and care of their children." It is also highly important to Seeds that the Mama Goddess Birth Shop promote products that are conducive to this vision and, as such, most of the shop's products are organic and natural. A true mother to everyone, she shares her love and birthing wisdom by stocking her shop full of smart, sustainable products such as herbal teas, natural care products, home birth kits, and homeopathic remedies specific to birthing. Says Seeds, "What we are doing is absolutely unique, not because it is the first, but because of how we are doing it."

Seeds provides parents-to-be with informed choices, not answers. "There is no right or wrong way to birth," she says, "nor is there any one way that will work for everyone."

Tel: 604.738.1543 | Cell: 604.782.6679 | Email: lotusbirth@shaw.ca
www.mamagoddessbirthshop.com | www.seedsofbirth.com

Mark Ainley

One Brain Facilitator and Instructor,
Contemporary Feng Shui Consultant,
Structure-Function Consultant

"Everything around you reflects something back to you—each part of your home represents an aspect of your life, your artwork sets the tone for your life experience, and your body reveals your life history." Mark Ainley, a contemporary feng shui consultant and practitioner of the One Brain system of body-mind integration, uses the principles of feng shui, applied kinesiology and behavioural genetics to make sense of it all for his clients. He helps them understand their life patterns and how to make shifts, whether it's shifting their furniture and artwork (feng shui) or shifting their belief systems (One Brain/Structure-Function).

One Brain is a system that helps individuals integrate body, mind and spirit so that they can make healthier choices. "Our past experience and choices influence how we view the world," says Ainley, "and the body-mind holds important information about how we respond to that world. When we release outmoded response patterns, we can experience life more fully." With the One Brain approach, information is accessed through muscle-testing and a system called Structure-Function. An offshoot of behavioural genetics, Structure-Function explores how the genetic structure of our body serves as a filter for information coming in and going out. "Understanding how these filters are 'programmed' is a major key to tuning in to our strengths and challenges", says Ainley.

Although he originally trained in the traditional Chinese approach to feng shui, Ainley has shifted to a more contemporary approach that he feels is simpler, more effective and more applicable to modern-day living. "You and your environment are one, whether you know it or not," he says, "and aligning your space with every aspect of your life helps you to co-exist with the world more gracefully." Ainley teaches and consults throughout North America, Europe and Japan.

Tel: 604.915.9464 | **Email:** mark@markainley.com | **www.markainley.com**

McIvor and Company

Olivia McIvor
Author, Human Resources Consultant, Training and Leadership Facilitator

To Olivia McIvor, achieving success as a company is simple: In order to stay competitive, companies must put the 'human' back into human resources. An HR consultant and leadership facilitator with over two decades of experience, McIvor helps clients see the crucial importance of linking employee health and well-being to the bottom line. "We need to learn that it is acceptable to take the whole person to work—all of who we are, our talents and gifts— and not just our skills. Companies can no longer avoid dealing with what we call the 'soft' issues such as stress, training and employee morale," she says. "Research shows that neglecting these issues is significantly debilitating to people, productivity and, consequently, profits—and with no profits, no company."

In her book, *The Business of Kindness: Creating Work Environments Where People Thrive*, McIvor discusses how today's workplace needs to focus on becoming healthy in order to stay competitive— particularly with the realities of resource shortages, downsizing, multiple roles, increased hours, and greater responsibility that companies face today. "One of the most noticeable and alarming effects of the increasing demands in the workplace is a greater propensity towards stress, and even violence," she says. "Both of these conditions inevitably lead to higher staff turnover, absenteeism, increased disability claims, lawsuits and, worst of all, a decrease in employee morale and engagement."

McIvor's workplace development programs combat the negative effects companies experience when they do not think holistically. Using unique, practical, hands-on techniques, she helps co-workers see the importance of placing positive emphasis on building their character and personal well-being, as well as on their professional development. Her simple advice for anyone from the frontline to the boardroom is to "be the change you want to see in your workplace. Take accountability and responsibility for your actions. Do yourself a favour: refuse to give less than 100%."

305 – 1591 West 16th Avenue | Vancouver, BC | V6J 2L7
Tel: 604.688.7809 | Email: mcivorconsulting@telus.net | www.inspirationalhr.com

Meru Mountain Meditation and Yoga

Janis Goad
Founder and Owner, Yoga Teacher, Columnist

Located in Burnaby, BC, Meru Mountain Meditation and Yoga offers courses in various levels of Hatha Flow and beginners Sivananda Yoga, as well as special classes for seniors, prenatal moms, and moms with their babies. In addition to offering classes at Meru, owner Janis Goad provides extensive community outreach services locally and long distance. Goad leads nourishing yoga vacations; guests travel to a resort destination to enjoy daily yoga, relaxation and exploration of the local culture. She also offers a series of yoga DVDs for various levels of practice—gentle, beginning, intermediate and advanced—available via her website, in local stores and at the Meru studio.

Goad initially learned about yoga 25 years ago at a meditation retreat in a Thai monastery. Her first encounter with postures such as Plough (Halasana) and Standing Forward Fold (Uttanasana) left her electrified by powerful energy running through her body and free of deep-seated tension. For the past 20 years, she has practiced and taught yoga and meditation to help clients move into inner stillness and to cultivate a healthy body, balance, radiance and inner stillness. Her goal is to heal and help others connect with their deepest levels of being, fostering compassion, wisdom and peace.

Her outreach services include teaching meditation and yoga in community centres, schools, to seniors, and in restorative yoga classes to people with multiple sclerosis, cancer or physical conditions that make participation in a regular yoga class unsuitable. The community-outreach classes include the beginners Hatha Flow, a meditative, flowing series of easy yoga poses for beginners. It has many seated and lying down poses (asanas) and introduces basic standing ones, as well as yogic breathing (pranayama) and guided relaxation. Through the practice of asanas or physical postures, mauna or choiceful restraint of speech, and chanting mantras such as 'om', yoga helps channel universal energy, creating a powerful thought form for peace and restorative health.

103 – 8686 Centaurus Circle | Burnaby, BC | V3J 7J9 | **Tel:** 604.421.8295
Cell: 778.388.8295 | **Email:** janisg@look.ca | **www.merumountainyoga.com**

Milagro Retreats

Shani Cranston
Holistic Chef, Organic Farmer,
Multi-Modality Practitioner

At 18 years of age, Shani Cranston embarked on a path towards holistic living, alternative medicine and yoga, which culminated in the establishment of Milagro Retreats—a Vancouver Island-based wellness company that offers all-inclusive retreat packages. When she moved to "10 acres of forested paradise," Cranston's vision of a place to nourish others began to grow. Equipped with an abundance of talent and a passion to share knowledge, Cranston gave birth to Milagro Retreats. To run this grassroots business, she draws upon her expertise as a holistic chef, a practitioner of multiple bodywork modalities, and an organic farmer. She and her partner, Willy McBride, continue to work towards a self-sustaining existence, growing their own food and using low-impact construction practices. Most of the organic produce served at Milagro's Summer Retreats in BC is grown on their farm in the Cowichan Valley.

"At Milagro Retreats, we believe in creating a sacred space where guests are encouraged to explore their full potential through movement, breath, Mother Nature, and Prana-infused cuisine," says Cranston. "We specialize in international yoga, surf retreats and organic vegetarian catering, embodying the slow food movement concepts." Milagro creates customized holistic experiences in a plethora of locations including Vancouver Island, Costa Rica and Baja, Mexico. Their yoga and surf retreats offer different forms of bodywork including deep tissue massage, craniosacral therapy, Reiki and the Trager approach. Their retreats also offer many additional activities, including Feldenkrais, five-rhythms dance, belly dance and transformational breath. "By experiencing many modalities and nourishing our bodies with healthy whole foods, we can dissolve our boundaries, enhance our awareness and ultimately realize unity with the source."

In the works is a line of healthy, organic snack foods from Milagro Retreats, which will be available in the near future. Milagro also supports other grassroots companies through an international network accessible via their website.

PO Box 737 | Lake Cowichan, BC | V0R 2G0
Email: info@milagroretreats.com | www.milagroretreats.com

Nao Isobel Sims

Creative Movement Teacher

The first time Nao Sims had the privilege of participating in a creative dance class, she was moved to tears as she witnessed women who had been dancing together for 20 years, "move like a flock of birds, flying across the sky. There was such freedom, such joy and companionship, that my heart threatened to swallow me up in its openness!"

Now, as a facilitator of creative dance classes for women, Sims believes that free-form authentic movement helps to support the healing of both the emotional and the physical body. "Creative dance gives us the opportunity to joyfully connect body, mind and spirit in beautiful ways. In my classes, we look to the natural world for guidance. We ask the elemental energies of earth, water, fire and air to support us, as we journey inward and then outward, as we relate to one another." She sincerely hopes that, through the dance, women might be able to move into a place that is "free of the obstructions of the judging mind and the paralyzing effects of self-consciousness, that they may have the opportunity to discover something wonderful about who they are, after moving freely for a while."

Sims explains that, for her, connecting our hearts to our heads in honest ways cannot help but deeply affect our unconscious. "Some people do it through meditation, I do it through dance. People have all kinds of delightful ways of learning about who they are, but this is my favourite." Her perception of living has been deeply affected by her experience in creative movement. What is her vision of the world? "I like to focus on celebration, dancing and singing, moving and grooving in all kinds of fun ways. This planet is just too beautiful to not."

Tel: 604.709.8005 | **Email:** naosims@telus.net

Nature's Path Organic Foods

Jyoti Stephens
Head of Sustainability

From its humble roots in a small organic berry farm on Vancouver Island in the 1950s, Nature's Path has become North America's largest certified organic cereal company. One of the few remaining independently owned and operated organic food companies of its size, it is backed by three generations of commitment to organic foods and farming. Its co-founder and president, Arran Stephens, is an artist, author and environmentalist who was raised on sound values, organic food and a deep respect for the earth. Embracing the principles of social progressiveness and environmental excellence, Stephens is "committed to producing products that support the development and sustenance of organic agriculture, while minimizing our ecological footprint and maintaining social, environmental and financial integrity."

In the spirit of the company's mission statement—to nurture people, nature and spirit—Stephens and his wife/co-founder Ratana recognized the need for someone to officially champion sustainability and social responsibility. Their daughter, Jyoti Stephens, has taken this task to heart, working with cross-departmental teams to help the company achieve its goals of minimizing environmental impact and creating zero waste. To this end, it runs a composting program to reduce waste and provide fertilizer for its organic staff gardens in Richmond; it promotes the use of renewable sources of power and carbon sequestration; to reduce wasteful packaging, it uses bulk 'eco pacs' for most cereals, has reduced the box size of most of its cereals by 10%, and always uses recycled cardboard; and it has even installed skylights in its head office to save on electricity and provide natural light for its employees.

"Sustainability is the key to our survival as a people, a society and a company," says Stephens. "At Nature's Path, we envision ourselves as leaders respectfully moving towards a healthier, more secure world. We want to help leave the planet better than we found it."

9100 Van Horne Way | Richmond, BC | V6X 1W3 | **Tel:** 1.888.808.9505
Email: sustainability@naturespath.com | **www.naturespath.com**

Ocean Wise

A Vancouver Aquarium Conservation Program

Empowering consumers to make sustainable seafood choices when shopping or dining out, the Ocean Wise program is the Vancouver Aquarium's latest conservation initiative. The program pairs the aquarium's marine conservation expertise with restaurants and chefs keen to include sustainable seafood options on their menus. Following a menu assessment, restaurants can join the program by removing one 'unsustainable' item from their menu and highlighting at least one 'sustainable' seafood item with an Ocean Wise logo. By looking for the logo on menus at participating restaurants and retailers, consumers can choose seafood that is guaranteed to have been sustainably harvested and ocean-friendly.

"Our objective is to foster a community of chefs and food industry workers who believe in sustainable seafood and are concerned about the conservation of the oceans," says Ocean Wise Coordinator, Mike McDermid. "We also want to make it easier for consumers to choose sustainable seafood and to understand the impact of their choices on the ocean environment." Sustainable seafood choices are those species that are abundant and resilient to fishing pressures, well managed with a comprehensive management plan, and harvested using a method that ensures limited by-catch and minimal habitat destruction.

Together with the Pacific Institute of Culinary Arts and Capers Community Markets, there are now more than 40 participating restaurants that have removed at least one non-sustainable item from their menu and are committed to removing at least one more every six months. Each restaurant chooses the level of commitment they can make, be it a fully sustainable menu or a handful of ocean-friendly choices for their customers. "The people we work with at participating restaurants and markets are dedicated to making a difference," says McDermid, "and they are integral to the future of our oceans." With Ocean Wise providing a user-friendly way for us all to make choices that have a positive impact on our oceans, now you can have your fish and eat it.

L-R: Jason Boyce, Tara Taylor, Executive Chef Robert Clark, C Restaurant, Mike McDermid

Robert Clark
Executive Chef

PO Box 3232 | Vancouver, BC | V6B 3X8 | **Tel:** 604.659.3596 | **Fax:** 604.659.3515
Email: oceanwise@vanaqua.org | **www.oceanwisecanada.org** | **www.vanaqua.org**

Olga Sheean

Relationship/Life Coach, Applied Kinesiologist,
Author, Writer, Speaker, Workshop Facilitator

"There is no denying the power of our mastery," claims relationship coach Olga Sheean. "We are the ones who, through fear, need or desire, create the scenarios we call life." Unfortunately, many people are unaware that they have such creative powers—and that's where Sheean comes in. She helps people transform their lives, by identifying their subconscious programming and showing them how it distorts their perception and the way they relate to themselves and others. Then, using muscle-testing to determine exactly what is going on inside, she provides clients with practical tools and techniques for creating the love, life and well-being that they want.

"My work provides a system for decoding life's scenarios, in the context of what is going on inside us, so that we can literally change our circumstances," says Sheean. Her personalized programs are truly holistic, encompassing nutrition, health, lifestyle, career issues and whatever else may be blocking an individual's success or fulfilment. Her illustrated book, *Fit for Love—find your self and your perfect mate*, shows how every relationship plays a key role in our personal evolution, taking us on a journey of self-discovery, healing and personal empowerment. "Anyone who affects us emotionally represents an opportunity for us to access and express more of ourselves," she says, "and it is in that fuller self-expression that our real power emerges."

Sheean developed her unique processes over a decade of personal study and private practice, analyzing interpersonal dynamics, the body-mind connection and the powerful impact of negative subconscious programming. Now, she works internationally, offering private consultations, coaching, workshops, seminars and "dream teams" (a unique group coaching process), dedicated to helping people transform their relationships, health, finances and happiness quotient. "Their empowerment is hugely inspiring," she says, "and it fuels the deep conviction I have in our ability to live magical lives."

Tel: 604.638.0772 | **Cell:** 604.999.8429
Email: insideout@olgasheean.com | **www.olgasheean.com**

Orineida Counselling Services

Leslie Williamson
Workshop Facilitator, Trainer, Counsellor

A one-woman powerhouse who travels across Canada, Leslie Williamson is a facilitator/trainer and counsellor promoting personal empowerment and healing. She is the owner and founder of Orineida Counselling Services, offering workshops that enable individuals and communities to embrace change through emotional and spiritual growth. A member of the Old Crow Band in the Yukon Territory, and trained by contemporary as well as First Nations teachers, Williamson has been involved in Aboriginal training and healing work since 1993. She believes that there is room for all races of people to live and work together in respectful, connecting ways. Her clients include corporate leaders, groups and individuals from all races, as well as First Nations chiefs and council members.

Williamson integrates native wisdom and healing rituals into her professional workshops, which include team-building, relationship-building, nonviolent communication skills, healing unresolved trauma, managing your power, and positive parenting. Fundamental to her work is the promotion of nonviolence. "When we can stop being violent towards ourselves, we will automatically stop being violent towards others," she says. She sees personal growth as an opportunity to transform a life of pain into a life of joy, peace and connection with one's higher self.

When working, Williamson cultivates an atmosphere of acceptance for her clients—creating an environment where participants can relax and open their minds along with their hearts to making positive changes. She shows others how to address and overcome life's challenges, demonstrating how each one represents an opportunity for growth and lasting, positive change. Having lived through her fair share of pain and disappointment, Williamson can still see the beauty in others and have compassion for those who express their pain in harmful ways. "We have all been harmful to self or another in this lifetime," she says, "and extending heartfelt compassion to others can transform their lives."

PO Box 902 | Vernon, BC | V1T 6M8 | **Tel:** 250.549.4707
Fax: 250.503.3042 | **Email:** gwitchen@hotmail.com | **www.lesliewilliamson.net**

Pacific Coast Naturopathic Centre

Dr Paula Fainstat, DC, ND
Naturopathic Physician

Dr Paula Fainstat is the founder and director of the Pacific Naturopathic Centre, which offers a wide range of medical and healing services including an innovative detoxification program. Her patients receive highly personalized treatment regimens. "Each patient is evaluated for the links between their symptom pattern, their optimal goals and their underlying health issues," she says. "Then a program is developed to address the patient's specific needs." Dr Fainstat's treatments address the physical, mental and emotional needs of her patients. The potential harmful effects of heavy metals, environmental toxins, chronic infections and allergies are always considered in her diagnostics and the treatments are adapted to the priorities of the healing process, as well as to the patient's lifestyle.

An innovative therapeutic program of the Pacific Naturopathic Centre is the Naturopathic Constitutional Drainage. As adequate tissue drainage is essential for all the body's systems to function properly and detoxify, this program offers patients an easy and comfortable therapy that includes a footbath with infrared heat, special clays, ozone, individually assessed herbs and homeopathics. Other popular programs include the Quick Release Technique for muscle rebalancing, Polyintegrative Technique for psychological repatterning and clearing, and Naturopathic Facial Rejuvenation for facial toning and drainage.

Dr Fainstat is proud of the history of her profession. British Columbia licensed and recognized the naturopathic medical profession in 1921, and the BC Naturopathic Association has been an active champion for the integration of complementary medicine into all levels of healthcare. The naturopathic doctors in this province have established a contemporary and progressive scope of practice drawn from skills as primary care physicians.

312 – 2083 Alma Street | Vancouver, BC | V6R 4N6 | Tel: 604.222.2433
Email: info@naturopathicdocs.com | www.naturopathicdocs.com

Pacific Institute of Reflexology

Christopher Shirley
Founder and Director, Reflexologist

Almost everyone knows how good a foot massage feels, but few know just how beneficial it can be for their health and well-being. Director of the Pacific Institute of Reflexology, Christopher Shirley is also a reflexologist whose mission is to bring the practice of reflexology into the social and medical mainstream. "Our society is largely dominated by the medical model and medical interpretations of sickness," says Shirley, "and it's time to heal the healthcare system by putting individuals' needs first and fostering greater integration between natural and modern medicine."

A teacher and practitioner of reflexology since 1978, Shirley has trained thousands of students through his courses. "Reflexology is essentially an intuitive healing art," he says, "and developing one's intuitive sense is a lifelong process." For Shirley, reflexology is an extremely simple, yet potent, therapy that has no negative side effects. It involves applying pressure to areas on the client's feet, hands or ears to stimulate specific organs, glands or body parts. Although there are several theories as to how reflexology works—by boosting the body's energy flow, the electrical field, the nervous system and/or the lymphatic system—the end result is deep relaxation and enhanced well-being.

In his ongoing commitment to generating greater acceptance of reflexology, Shirley produces and disseminates reflexology research through the Institute's reference library. He also sells books, reflexology charts, instructional DVDs/videos, and portable reclining chairs to meet students' and practitioners' needs. Current plans include a network of Pacific Institute of Reflexology natural healing schools and clinics, which will be available as franchise opportunities to like-minded individuals.

And the rewards for such commitment? "My greatest satisfaction comes from watching people melt as they receive reflexology, and, hearing my students report how their treatments produce seemingly miraculous results."

535 West 10th Avenue | Vancouver, BC | V5Z 1K9 | **Tel:** 604.875.8818 or 1.800.688.9748
Fax: 604.875.8868 | **Email:** chrisshirley@pacificreflexology.com | **www.pacificreflexology.com**

Paddi Moore

Jyotishi/Neo-Vedic Astrologer,
Healer, Speaker

Jyotisha, or Vedic astrology, is the language of the planets and the metaphysical science of timing, and Paddi Moore is both a messenger and a guide. She uses astrology as an agent for emotional and psychological healing with her clients, serving as a guide for their life journey. Astrological consultations act as a fundamental tool in the process of self-discovery and self-understanding. Jyotisha is the science of light and the language, if read by a spiritual non-judgmental being, directly assists one along the path to enlightenment.

Moore graduated from the Astrological Faculty of England in 1987 and recently earned a Bachelor of Arts degree in Jyotisha from the American College of Vedic Astrologers. She combines many different forms of readings into her spiritual practice, including astronomy, mathematics, birth chart calculation, and astrological answers based on the questions why and when. "I interpret this language for clients in a direct, yet gentle, manner and I stay with them for life whenever they need to consult the wisdom this language holds. It is my honour to be gifted with the insight and grace to be a channel for this body of knowledge," she says.

While Moore offers intense personal transformation coaching for those wishing to make a quantum leap in consciousness, she can vision for more than individuals. "I can feel a vortex spinning around the Vancouver area," she says of her hometown. "I believe it is a protected centre for light to enter the planet and cause a positive evolution in humanity." Moore accepts speaking engagements on a variety of topics, including astrology, self-realization, transformation of self in business, corporate profiling, stress management and New Age spirituality. Readings are taped and highly confidential. Moore is committed to professionalism and holds a high regard for individual spirituality. She is a qualified teacher/tutor of Vedic astrology, and a member of the American Council of Vedic Astrologers.

Tel: 778.988.8808 | Email: love@uniserve.com
www.inner-dynamics.com | www.myenergywatch.com

Pamela Stroud, RA

Registered Aromatherapist

Pamela Stroud is a Registered Aromatherapist with a passion for, and extensive experience in, essential oil therapy. A trusted friend and professional mentor introduced her to the medicinal properties and values of essential oils many years ago. The insights gained from her study of aromatherapy started her on a journey to personal wellness and led to the establishment of her professional practice. Since then, Stroud has undergone extensive training in many facets of holistic healing—reflexology, healing touch and colon hydrotherapy. Combining her love for essential oils with a passion for encouraging and mentoring others, she has dedicated herself to the development of effective tools for use in the aromatherapy industry. "I love watching clients learn how to use essential oils for themselves," says Stroud. "There are so many success stories that testify to the miraculous healing power of these beautiful, natural healing substances!"

An active member of the British Columbia Association of Aromatherapists and the British Columbia Alliance of Aromatherapy, Stroud is committed to ensuring the highest standards in her healing practice. For her fellow professionals, she recently developed the *Aromatherapy Tool Kit: Blending by Condition*, a quick and easy method of creating highly effective essential oil blends for the practice of aromatherapy. Says Stroud, "I am proud to be part of a group of professionals who have worked tirelessly for years to establish the practice of aromatherapy as a recognized profession, in addition to promoting professional, measurable and consistent educational standards."

She is encouraged to find healers of every kind joining in the spirit of unity: "Individually, we can do so little but, together, it becomes so much more! Just like aromatherapy blending—one essential oil is good, but several blended together synergistically can produce miraculous results in healing the body, mind and spirit."

4105 – 256 Street | Aldergrove, BC | V4W 1X1 | **Tel:** 604.857.0765
Cell: 604.308.9476 | **Fax:** 604.857.0765 | **Email:** stroudoffice@yahoo.ca | **www.aromatherapytoolkit.com**

The Pilates Den Wellness Studio

Emmie Li, BA
Certified Gold Level Teacher
by The Pilates Method Alliance

The creator of the Pilates method, Joseph Pilates, claimed that people could feel a difference in their body after 10 Pilates sessions. In 20 sessions, he said, people would see the difference and, in 30, they would have a whole new body. Every day, Emmie Li witnesses the wisdom of his claims, whether in her own personal practice or through the progress of her clients. The result of effective Pilates work is remarkable strength, flexibility and empowerment. "Whether your goals are rehabilitative or weight-loss-based, Pilates' unique body-conditioning program will transform your mind and body forever," says Li.

Pilates, a German-born athlete and physical-therapy pioneer, believed that physical fitness was the first requisite of happiness. He defined physical fitness as "the attainment and maintenance of a uniformly developed body with a sound mind fully capable of naturally, easily and satisfactorily performing our many and varied daily tasks with spontaneous zest and pleasure."

Li offers her clients the benefits of 12 years of experience in Pilates programming, including exclusive training with renowned international Pilates elders. She studied privately with the legendary Mary Bowen who learned from Joseph Pilates himself. Li also draws on her knowledge in yoga and classical ballet to develop comprehensive programs for her clients, providing her unique methodologies in small groups or private sessions that allow her to work closely and intensively with them. She sees not only physical improvements in her clients, but also the mental transformation the practice of Pilates can create. "Movement patterns are influenced by our thoughts and emotions," says Li. "By learning to move in a graceful alignment, my clients develop a healthy mind and spirit, and become empowered to move through their lives with ease and integrity."

205 – 4250 Kingsway | Burnaby, BC | V5H 4T7 | Tel: 604.431.3818
Fax: 604.432.1301 | Email: thepilatesden@yahoo.com | www.thepilatesden.com

The Pinch Group at Raymond James Ltd*

Passionate Ethical Investors

L-R, Back to Front: Mark Duncan, Frank Arnold, Brian Pinch, Lori Woytowich, Michael Higgins

Led by Brian Pinch, who has over 20 years' experience as a financial advisor, the Pinch Group is a highly skilled team of financial advisors committed to socially responsible investing (SRI). SRI empowers individuals to make a positive impact in the world by investing the power of their wealth into companies whose operations, products and services are aligned with their personal values. The idea is not to replace conventional investing, but rather to enhance it by adding social, ethical and environmental criteria.

"If we are committed to positive change, we must use all the tools we have at our disposal, including the power of our investments, to support these changes," says Pinch. "And since SRI rewards the leaders, punishes the laggards and engages those in between, it is a powerful tool in all directions."

A Fellow of the Canadian Securities Institute (one of the highest certifications in the investment industry), Pinch has been a pioneer in the development of SRI in Canada—as a result of his own negative experiences with unethical companies. "Avoiding such companies felt good," he says, "but seeking out companies that matched my values was even more rewarding." Currently entrusted with more than $90 million worth of institutional and private assets for his clients, Pinch is poised to take SRI to a wider audience in BC, Alberta and Ontario. He credits the independent and entrepreneurial culture at Raymond James Ltd (which he joined five years ago) for setting the foundation for his team, which now provides expertise and advice in financial planning, estate planning and charitable gift planning.

"The most rewarding part of our job is not just helping people reach their financial goals," says Pinch, "but enabling them to do so with a clean conscience and in a way that has a positive social and environmental impact."

1000 – 1175 Douglas Street | Victoria, BC | V8W 2E1 | **Fax:** 250.405.2499
Tel: 250.405.2468 or 1.877.405.2400 | **Email:** pinchgroup@raymondjames.ca
www.pinchgroup.ca | *Raymond James Ltd is a member of the Canadian Investor Protection Fund.*

81

L-R, Back to Front: Peter Wrinch, David Eby, Paul Ryan, Viki Jackson, John Richardson, Karin Stredulinsky, Wilfred Chan, Alvin Lau, Aasma Ahmad

Pivot Legal Society

Advocacy Through Legal Action

A non-profit legal advocacy organization located in Vancouver's Downtown Eastside, Pivot Legal Society takes a strategic approach to social change, using the law to address the root causes undermining the lives of those on the margins. Focusing on addiction, housing, policing and sex work, it advances the interests of marginalized persons through law reform, legal education and strategic legal action.

"We believe that everyone, regardless of income, benefits from a healthy and inclusive community where values such as opportunity, respect and equality are strongly rooted in the law," says Pivot's co-founder John Richardson. The basic concept underlying Pivot's name and mission is that a critical pressure point of social change is to be found at the lower edge of legal and social boundaries. By systematically challenging the attitudes and institutions of power that enable marginalization, and using the media to boost public awareness, Pivot helps create a more tolerant, inclusive and compassionate society.

Pivot's key values—personal empowerment, integrity and compassion—keep the focus on the causes of problems rather than the symptoms. Pivot views itself not as merely providing legal services as a charity for the poor, but as a lawyer committed to its clients, taking informed direction from them and creating opportunities for them to take control of their lives and make healthier choices. Over the next five years, Pivot will establish a social enterprise legal cooperative with a mission to foster a new generation of lawyers dedicated to a principled approach to law and a commitment to social justice. By hiring co-op lawyers, clients will help marginalized people in the Downtown Eastside as the profits will go towards Pivot's community work. Every dollar Pivot spends on staff time is matched by approximately $10 worth of time donated by more than 100 pro bono lawyers, researchers, writers, organizers and other volunteers.

678 East Hastings Street | Vancouver, BC | V6A 1R1 | **Tel:** 604.255.9700
Fax: 604.255.1552 | **Email:** info@pivotlegal.org | **www.pivotlegal.org**

Pomegranate Community Midwives

Lehe Elarar and Kat Montgomery
Founders

L-R: Lehe Elarar, Kat Montgomery

Throughout history, all over the world, there is a rich legacy of women helping women through pregnancy, the birthing process, and in all stages of child rearing. Although Canada was one of the last countries in the developed world to recognize the practice of midwifery, in the mid-1990s, British Columbia established the College of Midwives of BC and, in 1998, the first registered midwives began to practice the ancient service. Midwives are part of a community of allied health and maternity care professionals dedicated to creating a safe and satisfying experience for mothers and babies. Their services are covered by BC Medical and they are proud to provide clients with a choice of birthplace: home or hospital.

Pomegranate Community Midwives, in the heart of East Vancouver, opened in 2006. It provides a diverse practice of registered midwives who create an empowering environment where clients are respected, informed and included as active decision-makers. "Midwives recognize pregnancy and birth as a significant, healthy and dynamic part of a woman's life," says Lehe Elarar, a registered midwife with the clinic. "We offer sensitive and expert care from conception to six weeks postpartum, including complete labour and birth care." The women of Pomegranate offer their services in five languages and, with respect to the diversity of their neighbourhoods, feel privileged to offer care to women of many different cultural backgrounds.

Pomegranate's goal for the next five years is to continue to improve and expand services for women, children and families in a forward-thinking community that empowers and supports clients. Creating a family is a social statement. The midwives at Pomegranate have created a space where discussing the political, social and cultural context of family life, in whatever structure it is presented, is openly explored.

2647 East Hastings Street | Vancouver, BC | V5K 1Z5 | **Tel:** 604.255.5556
Fax: 604.255.5576 | **Email:** office@pomegranate-midwives.com | **www.pomegranate-midwives.com**

The Positive Rebel

Michael Bortolotto
Motivational Speaker

How does a speech-impaired little boy grow up to be an inspirational and life-changing public speaker? "Raw courage and sheer determination," says Michael Bortolotto, who was born with cerebral palsy. Michael, who has delivered over 1,000 speeches before more than 250,000 people, encourages audiences by recounting his personal struggles and achievements. "I believe my purpose in life is to motivate, inspire and educate people by drawing on the unique challenges created by my cerebral palsy. I have turned those challenges into opportunities and live life with an 'I can do it attitude'. I know that, given the correct tools, others can do it too."

After graduating from Malaspina University-College in 1987, Bortolotto pursued his goal of becoming a motivational speaker. He cites his mother as the motivation in his own life: "My mom always believed in my abilities and taught me how to move beyond challenges and limitations. She taught me that there are no limitations to the mind except for those we accept." In his talks, he urges his audience not to be afraid of change. "To gain the most from life we must constantly stretch and strive to reach our full potential," says Bortolotto, and he encourages people to stretch past personal comfort levels and continue to embrace new ideas and concepts. He believes that by rebelling with courage, conviction and effective thinking, goals can be achieved in one's personal life while providing support to others in achieving theirs.

Known as The Positive Rebel, Bortolotto has worked with many associations, frontline staff, corporations, government organizations, athletes, realtors, bankers and school children, to name a few. "I strive to empower people, regardless of age, to make positive changes in how they feel, think and act when encountering various life-prohibiting obstacles, and how to face challenges head on and be a 'positive rebel'. "

Bortolotto & Associates | **Tel:** 250.483.6779 | **Email:** michael@positiverebel.ca | **www.positiverebel.ca**

Power On Chiropractic

Dr Heidi Benda, BAA, DC
Doctor of Chiropractic

Dr Heidi Benda is a purposeful chiropractic doctor and healer who loves her patients. She believes that the power that made the body is the power that heals the body. When Dr Benda works with her clients she uses her hands to adjust their spinal column, resulting in restored nerve flow and enhanced communication between the brain and the body. The restored flow in the nervous system, the master system in the body, promotes healing and well-being. While her hands are her tools, she is tuned in and focused on the needs of each client. "When I work with my clients, I am in a state of 100% pure energy to affect each person for the better," she says. "My ideal client is someone who wants to maximize their performance and optimize their health."

As a holistic and therapeutic practitioner, Dr Benda not only witnesses the disappearance of illness, but also sees remarkable improvements in her patients' entire well-being. She says, "as the function in people's spines improve, so do their lives. My patient's relationships with themselves, their families, acquaintances and community also improve. It continually impresses me to witness how a very specific controlled motion given with the right intention can have such a massive positive effect on a person and set in motion greater health, vitality, happiness and 'well-being'.

Healing others is only one aspect of a larger and deeper commitment that Dr Benda has to her spiritual calling. She is also involved with Chiropractors with Compassion, a national organization affiliated with Compassion International, which helps children in need globally, through agriculture development, education and healthcare programs. Dr Benda also gives regular workshops throughout the year to educate her community on how to turn the healing power back on in the body.

905 – 16th Street West | North Vancouver, BC | V7P 1R2 | **Tel:** 604.929.7700
Email: info@poweronchiropractic.com | **www.poweronchiropractic.com**

Rae Armour

Real Estate Agent, BioPro Technology Consultant, Sunrider Distributor, Musician and Performing Artist

Rae Armour is a realtor, musician and wellness entrepreneur whose role is to educate and inspire people to create excellent financial and life decisions. Her muses are both 'right brain' (singing, songwriting, performing) and 'left brain' (real estate and promoting wellness products such as BioPro Technology and Sunrider). "Existing in many circles is the model for success that I follow," she says.

Armour is a successful, award-winning realtor in the Greater Vancouver area and works with BioPro Technology to protect clients from electro-pollution. Her involvement with BioPro Technology is a direct result of her knowledge about the health hazards caused by electromagnetic fields and cell phones, believed to disrupt the sensitive signals with which our brains and nervous systems communicate, resulting in allergies, illnesses and deteriorating health. She shares the solution to this problem with her fellow realtors and others whose use of cell phones is extensive. As a realtor, she has defined her own way of doing business, working largely by referral and, as a result, has satisfied homeowners on the North Shore, Downtown, in East Vancouver and on the West Side. For the past 13 years, she has taught a popular workshop at the West End Community Centre, Are You Tired of Renting?, which offers people a safe environment in which to ask questions and learn how to become a homeowner. "Teaching the course gives people the tools to better understand the steps to ownership," says Armour.

As for her singing career, which has inspired audiences for over 25 years, a recent highlight includes opening for Faith Hill at Whistler. "My work seems to revolve around cell phones, telephones and microphones," laughs Armour. Her new singing group, August, spotlights her singing talent, her wonderful sense of humour and her spiritual elegance. "My life's work lies in helping people to realize their dream of owning a home, of protecting their health against electro-pollution, and of hopefully opening their hearts through my music."

Cell: 604.240.2508 | Tel: 604.257.8333 | Email: aarmour@shaw.ca | www.raearmour.com
www.mybiopro.ca/raearmour | www.raearmourmusic.com | august-music.blogspot.com

Recycling Alternative

Robert Weatherbe and Louise Schwarz
Founders

In 1989, there were two passionate environmentalists with a new idea and a hatchback. Seventeen years later, Recycling Alternative business partners Robert Weatherbe and Louise Schwarz continue to successfully build upon their vision, and are proud to say that the hatchback has been replaced by a fleet of seven operating trucks, five of which are fueled by BioDiesel—an environmentally friendly, biodegradable transportation fuel for use in diesel engines. Recycling Alternative not only offers convenient, affordable recycling services to businesses throughout the Greater Vancouver area, it also helps fuel the movement and spread the popularity of recycling in the workplace.

Their prescient vision predates the 'blue box'. Back in the late 80s, there were very few environmentally responsible disposal options with a focus on recycling available to individuals and businesses. Recycling Alternative was founded to fill that need. The company offers services to all businesses, regardless of size, tailoring its services to suit the needs of small to medium-sized businesses that often don't meet the minimum volume requirements of other recycling service companies. "We want to make it easy and hassle-free for our clients to do their part for the environment in the workplace," says Weatherbe.

Over the last two years, Recycling Alternative has ventured into the world of BioDiesel. They were one of the first commercial fleets to operate trucks on BioDiesel and they currently manage and host the Vancouver BioDiesel Coop's pump on their worksite— the only pump to offer 100% BioDiesel in the city. From recycling visionaries in 1989 to BioDiesel visionaries in 2006, Weatherbe and Schwarz are thinking globally and acting locally. "With the choices our clients make in their businesses, they are an active part of environmental solutions, engaging with their community, and providing it with direction," they say. "It's all about taking action and being responsible."

L–R: Robert Weatherbe, Louise Schwarz

360 Industrial Avenue | Vancouver, BC | V6A 2R3 | **Tel:** 604.874.SAVE (7283)
Fax: 604.874.7252 | **Email:** recalt@telus.net | **www.recyclingalternative.com**

L-R: Anna Mannering, with client Rachel Davis

ReLeaf Natural Body Alignment

Anna Mannering
Alignment Trainer, Coach/Mentor,
Holistic Wellness Facilitator

Anna Mannering is dedicated to helping her clients reconnect mind, body and spirit through the practice of natural kinesiology. "What starts out as a simple pattern of response can become a neuro-muscular habit," explains Mannering. "Our body is always trying in earnest to communicate with us but we are often reticent to pay due attention. I help clients diagnose and correct problems caused by body misalignment."

Her practice is based on the principles of the natural kinesiology method founded in 2004 by her mentor, friend and teacher Gene Bausman. Through her training and many dedicated hours of practical experience, Mannering has become one of the first practitioners of this form of natural body alignment, offering her clients an opportunity to gently rebuild the structural and emotional integrity of their bodies for an improved, pain-free quality of life. "It is incredibly rewarding to know that I am helping people to help themselves," she says. "While developing a holistic awareness of the body's responses, people are able to gain relief from their pain. Seeing and hearing how they can once again do things with ease and flexibility that they haven't been able to do for months or, at times, years, is very satisfying."

True wellness requires taking time to re-establish communication with ones body so that the mind, body and spirit are all in balance. Mannering believes that practitioners of both traditional and alternative forms of medicine can develop unique complementary relationships and together create a physically and spiritually healthier world. "We are all one in the universal sense, and when we work for the good of the whole, rather than just the individual, then we become true visionaries."

Alternate Route Healing | 421 – 1033 Davie Street | Vancouver, BC | V6E 1M7 | **Tel:** 604.682.7413
Ladner Natural Health Clinic | 4861 Delta Street | Delta, BC | V4K 2T9 | **Tel:** 604.946.1424
Cell: 604.961.9155 | **Email:** anna@goldleafproductions.com

Renewal Partners Company and Endswell Foundation

Joel Solomon, President and Executive Director
Carol A. Newell, Founder and Funder

L–R: Carol Newell, Joel Solomon

Carol Newell and Joel Solomon are changing the way society thinks about capital, wealth and investment—key components of the consumer-driven economy in which we live. They are helping to change our economy into one that is socially and environmentally responsible, not just profit-driven. As founders of two organizations—Renewal Partners and the Endswell Foundation—they offer customized consulting and program-design support for individuals who want to commit their financial resources to the betterment of the world. "We support businesses and social profits that, together, can be leaders towards a model of social and environmental sustainability in British Columbia," says Solomon. "Through the growth of healthy jobs in companies and civic organizations, along with learning and networking opportunities," adds Newell, "a powerful and positive social change movement can be built in any region."

At Renewal Partners, Newell and Solomon work to provide seed capital for social-purpose companies, helping them to successfully grow and survive in business. The Endswell Foundation supports the environmental movement in BC by providing grants to selected projects. Together, they are building a base of independent and interdependent individuals and organizations committed to bringing forth a just and sustainable society. "Hopefully, our work serves to raise the bar for how financial resources can be used for more than strictly commercial purposes, so that others will be inspired to go further," says Solomon.

As for their advice on how to live a fully realized life personally, professionally and organizationally? "Determine how much money is 'enough' for you and your family, and then devote substantial resources beyond that amount to the causes you believe contribute the most to society. Further, do business with friends and those you love whenever possible, and cultivate practices that increase the success of those relationships. And, finally, vote with your dollars."

610 – 220 Cambie Street | Vancouver, BC | V6B 2M9 | **Tel:** 604.844.7474 | **Fax:** 604.844.7441
Email: info@renewalpartners.com | **www.renewalpartners.com** | **www.endswell.org**

Roundhouse Dental

Matthias Hammer, DMD, Dr med, Dr med dent
Holistic Dentist and Medical Doctor

Dr Matthias Hammer is a dentist who acknowledges and cares about his patients' mind, body and spirit—not just their teeth. He approaches his clients' health and safety from both a conventional standpoint and an alternative healthcare point of view. A dentist and a medical doctor, Dr Hammer practiced dentistry in Germany for over 10 years before he opened his office in Canada in 2003. "I consider dentistry to be an art form as well as a science," he says, "and I believe in integrating all traditional, holistic, alternative and conventional approaches to healing." With innovative ideas and the very latest in high-tech equipment, Dr Hammer ensures that visiting the dentist is a pleasant experience.

Offering all aspects of dental specialties—from cleaning, fillings, safe amalgam removal, oral surgery and implants, to esthetic and full-mouth reconstruction—Dr Hammer can accommodate all dentistry needs of his clients so that they do not have to consult different specialists around the city. He prides himself in providing individualized treatment solutions for everyone with his wide-ranging expertise in fixed and removable dentistry. And as an artist with a love for architecture, he has created an office that blends health and esthetics with quality and comfort.

Dr Hammer is a lover of life and learning. He takes an exuberant approach to living healthily and enjoys everything from kayaking to Latin dancing—while staying on the cutting edge of his profession by participating in dental study clubs and further education. His practice reflects his radiant personality, creating a positive personal environment in which he provides his patients with a great deal more that just dental treatment.

1286 Pacific Boulevard | Vancouver, BC | V6Z 2V1 | **Tel:** 604.806.6086 or 604.806.6087
Email: info@roundhousedental.com | **www.roundhousedental.com**

90

Ryan Carnahan, DCH, RMT

Homeopath and Registered Massage Therapist

Ryan Carnahan is "addicted to learning." Everything he's learned from both his spiritual teachers and his experiences travelling the world has expanded his mind and skill set. "I love travelling and have found enrichment in my journeys to Nepal, India, Japan and Thailand," he says. "Visiting other cultures gives me new perspectives and understandings about myself."

His spiritual and experiential learning has brought tremendous growth to his business as a Registered Massage Therapist and Homeopath. Since opening his practice in 1994, Carnahan's business has evolved from being primarily musculoskeletal-based to one that sees a full spectrum of health concerns—from depression and anxiety to immune and menopausal problems. Carnahan pairs his formal training with his intuitive senses to facilitate all-encompassing healing for his clients' mind, body and spirit. His practice is based on his post-graduate work in osteopathy, postural biomechanics, Bowen therapy, and advanced homeopathy and energy medicine. An advocate of self-healing, he believes that "by gaining knowledge, people can tap into their potential as human beings and experience their greatness that is just waiting to be explored."

For Carnahan, living in British Columbia—where there is a large holistic community and an open-mindedness for alternative therapies—is a blessing, but his practice is not limited by geography. He offers homeopathic consultations in person or by phone for those who don't have access to treatment or who are travelling. In addition to his practice, Carnahan also teaches workshops on health and wellness so people can learn how to heal themselves. "I really enjoy finding new ways in which I can help people. What I find the most rewarding is seeing people make changes in themselves and their lives. It's a real privilege to be a part of that."

Tel: 604.812.1190 | **Email:** rcarnahan@telus.net | **www.ryancarnahan.com**

Sacred Earth Journeys

Helen Tomei
Founder and President

"Travel is fatal to prejudice, bigotry and narrow-mindedness." Helen Tomei came to appreciate the essential, world-changing truth in these words by Mark Twain on journeys to far-flung corners of the globe with her father, who she describes as "an adventurer at heart." Tomei's own adventurous spirit still guides her and, in 2003, helped merge her passion for enlightening travel with a growing interest in spirituality, yoga and ancient traditions to create an innovative agency that seeks to help others explore their own new paths.

Sacred Earth Journeys develops special packages and tours around pursuits of increasing popularity and importance to many travellers, such as wellness, yoga, adventure and spiritual discovery. Assisted by her network of like-minded souls around the world, Tomei organizes unique, guided experiences through contemporary and traditional cultures at many of the most sacred sites in Bali, India, Ireland, Peru, Scotland and Sedona.

Though travel carriers and accommodations are comfortably modern, a Sacred Earth Journeys experience is often like a voyage back in time to examine rituals and healing practices among the pyramids of ancient Egypt or the temples of the Incas, Mayans and Toltecs of the central Americas, or to witness the celestial ceremonies of the Druids, Knights Templar and Celts of early Britain. "Imagine a group meditation inside the king's chamber in Egypt, or a private ceremony at Stonehenge, or perhaps a candlelit ceremony held in a natural cenote in the Yucatan," says Tomei. "It's hard to view the world the same way once you've participated in an Incan sunrise ceremony at Machu Picchu."

Yet, for all the mindful experiences and physical challenges offered by these global travel adventures, Tomei always adds something extra and, perhaps, even more valuable—the chance to relax, restore balance to life and rejuvenate body, mind and spirit.

220 – 133 East 8th Avenue | Vancouver, BC | V5T 1R8 | **Tel:** 604.874.7922 or 1.877.874.7922
Email: helen@sacredearthjourneys.ca | **www.sacredearthjourneys.ca**

Sage and Cedar

Sandra Molendyk, Dip Arts and Science, BA, GDBA
Intuitive Healer, Reiki Master, Shaman,
Certified LaStone Therapist

Whether an elite athlete, weekend warrior, parent or business executive, Sandra Molendyk is able to help clients excel in all levels of life. With her specialized treatments and workshops, Molendyk would like to "unleash the client's inner warrior". At the core of her healing is the ability to heal the heart and spirit. As a Shaman, she is called upon to mediate between the needs of people, forces of the spirit world, and the environment. For generations, the healers of her kind have been relied upon to cure disease, exorcise spirits, promote success in hunting and connect the body with the soul.

As a Sport Shaman and triathlete, Molendyk empowers athletes with unique treatments tailored to improve athletic performance, speed recovery from injury and training, eliminate pre-performance anxiety, and enhance the understanding of the athletes' mind, body and spirit connection. Providing resources and eye-opening lessons for all, Molendyk has clients around the world who recognize her advanced intuitive and shamanic healing abilities, distant healing and profound knowledge.

As an intuitive healer with healing hands and spirit, Molendyk is able to diagnose ethereal disturbances and encourage healing. She is a spirit-and-soul-recovery specialist with abilities that extend beyond traditional Reiki. "I feel, I see, I structure and I fix, creating concordance and harmony," she says. The benefits include awakening to one's inner wisdom, increased self-esteem, learning to trust one's gifts, spiritual and emotional healing, and a safer, more relaxed, pain-free life.

Her goal in life is to create harmony, joy and respect between people and the environment. While her degrees in environmental science and business have provided her with intellectual might, her true education has come from a much more in depth study of healing, and her power stems from her connection to nature.

202 – 3641 West 29th Avenue | Vancouver, BC | V6S 1T5 | Cell: 778.861.7243
Email: healing@sageandcedar.ca | www.sageandcedar.ca
Email: achieve@sportsshaman.com | www.sportsshaman.com

Saje Natural Wellness Stores and the Alchemy Network

Jean-Pierre LeBlanc, Relationship and Success Coach, Author, Speaker, Co-Founder of Saje

With a passion for holistic healing, a heart for humanity and a nose for business, Jean-Pierre LeBlanc is serving his life's mission of global wellness through two initiatives: the Saje Natural Wellness Stores and The Alchemy Network.

LeBlanc is co-founder of the retail chain Saje Natural Wellness Stores, which now includes nine Canadian locations and two international stores. The stores, for which franchising and licensing are available worldwide, feature over 400 therapeutic plant-based products that he personally formulated. He believes that exponential growth is ahead for holistic wellness methodologies and that everyone will want access to affordable, effective natural products and treatments. With a name chosen to reflect the natural healing powers of the sage plant as well as the wisdom of the sages in the philosophical sense, Saje has a large clientele who have discovered the great results of holistic healing, freeing themselves from pharmaceutical drugs and moving towards self-directed wellness.

LeBlanc is also a success coach and a professional speaker through the Alchemy Network, which was created for entrepreneurs around the globe wanting to learn, grow and network with like-minded individuals. Through intensive weekend workshops, Alchemy Network clients learn that every business issue is first a personal one. Participants experience how they can transform their lives, benefiting from peer mentorship, networking and coaching; clients regularly achieve miraculous results. LeBlanc's forte is "gender synergy"—he helps clients understand the masculine/feminine dynamic at play in all communication, and teaches systems that allow for extraordinary personal and professional results.

4515 Belmont Avenue | Vancouver, BC | V6R 1C5 | Tel: 604.709.3686
Fax: 604.709.3699 | Email: coach@saje.ca | www.saje.ca | www.thealchemynetwork.ca

Salt Spring Coffee

Mickey McLeod and Robbyn Scott
Certified Organic Fair Trade Coffee
Roasters, Wholesalers and Retailers

The folks at Salt Spring Coffee are brewing up quite the accomplishment. A successful local business that prides itself on its community roots, it proves that a company can be low impact and profitable. Salt Spring Coffee roasts 100% certified organic coffee, while making sure to pay Fair Trade prices. Partners Mickey McLeod and Robbyn Scott take great care in ensuring the handpicked organic beans are roasted with care to ensure freshness and great taste. "Our mission is to be an engaging leader, locally and globally, in providing premium quality, Fair Trade and Certified organic products to promote and support global sustainability."

McLeod and Scott are dedicated, ethically conscious professionals. They involve themselves in the production process by being committed to forming long-lasting relationships with the farmers. "It's a great reward to see the happiness expressed by the farmers when they welcome us to their coffee farms and share their appreciation for our support of their coffee, and the Fair Trade movement," says McLeod. On top of offering customers delicious organic coffee, Salt Spring Coffee is also an extremely environmentally conscious business. They reduce emissions by buying 100% BC Hydro Green Power; they operate with energy-efficient compact cars and bio-diesel delivery trucks; and they use 100% post-consumer waste paper, vegetable dye ink, and compact fluorescent lighting.

McLeod and Scott are proof that profit can co-exist with a commitment to their local Salt Spring Island community as well as to the global community. Their advice for all: "Embrace community, grow organically, buy locally, exercise and spend time walking in nature. Take time to enjoy a cup of fresh-roasted, organic Fair Trade coffee while bird-watching."

L-R: Mickey McLeod, Robbyn Scott

1 – 156 Alders Road | Salt Spring Island, BC | V8K 2K5 | **Tel:** 250.537.0805 | **Cell:** 250.537.7662
Fax: 250.537.8952 | **Email:** mickey@saltspringcoffee.com or robbyn@saltspringcoffee.com | **www.saltspringcoffee.com**

Sapphire Day Spa

Heidi Sherwood
Owner, Ayurvedic Therapist

Heidi Sherwood is passionate about health, wellness and making a positive contribution to her community. She believes that taking time out of our busy schedules to nurture ourselves is one of the golden keys to a long and happy life. She founded Sapphire Day Spa with a vision of providing a space where clients feel welcome, nurtured and free to be themselves. Located in the heart of downtown Victoria, the spacious spa is dedicated to providing rejuvenation, balance and lasting value. Sherwood has coined the term 'Eurovedic' to describe the spa's specialized treatments and consultations (which include esthetics, massage, body treatments and lifestyle wellness), as the services incorporate both classic Ayurvedic and European elements.

"Our uniqueness lies in our emphasis of the traditions and therapies of Ayurveda, a 5000-year-old health system that originated in India," says Sherwood. "In addition to offering the traditional European beauty services expected from spas, we incorporate the body treatments based on traditional medicine that aid in the treatment of disease and create balance in the body, giving radiance, improved health and a sense of well-being." The many benefits of Sapphire's Eurovedic treatments include improving blood circulation, balancing acne-prone skin, eliminating toxins, breaking down cellulite, reducing muscle spasm and increasing mobility, lowering blood pressure, reducing stress, and promoting relaxation.

Sherwood believes that intention is a powerful force. She inspires and nurtures clients, contributing to their well-being and enabling them to make positive contributions to their communities and to the earth. "I believe that I've witnessed miracles, have been celestially blessed and learned important life lessons at a young age," says Sherwood. "I continue to be inspired by dedicated people who speak their truth, laugh aloud and smile despite hardship."

714 View Street | Victoria, BC | V8W 1J8 | **Tel:** 250.385.6676
Fax: 250.385.6673 | **Email:** info@sapphiredayspa.com | **www.sapphiredayspa.com**

Semperviva Yoga Studios and Lifestyle Store

Gloria Latham, Founder, Director of Yoga Teacher Training, Yoga Teacher, Pharmacist

Voted Vancouver's best multidisciplinary yoga studio, Semperviva offers classes, workshops, retreats and teacher training in six different styles of yoga: Hatha, Ashtanga, Power, Yin, Kundalini and Pre-natal. Its founder, pharmacist and yoga teacher Gloria Latham, started Semperviva in 1995 to promote holistic health and to make yoga accessible to people of all ages and abilities. "I believe that yoga is for everybody and our classes cater to all levels of fitness and experience, in friendly, non-intimidating environments," says Latham.

Semperviva includes a specialized health centre and four yoga studios—the Sky, Sun, City and Sea Centres on Granville Island and Vancouver's West Side. Students can opt for a powerful workout, therapeutic practice or deep relaxation after a stressful day. In addition to ongoing classes and very comprehensive teacher-training programs, the studios offer workshops with local and world-renowned teachers. Weekly events include meditation, positive-living and couples workshops as well as introductory yoga classes and retreats. Latham also offers yoga retreats at her home on the Greek island of Kythera.

"People make positive life changes when they practice yoga. They take a proactive approach to their health" says Latham. With a diverse support team that includes pharmacists, doctors of Traditional Chinese Medicine, homeopaths and naturopaths, Semperviva also provides cleansing and detox kits, vitamins and herbals, homeopathic remedies, yoga accessories, books, CDs and natural skin care.

A dynamic, inspiring teacher who looks more like a 20-year-old than a just-turned-40 mother of two, Latham is a glowing example of what yoga can do for a body. "Try our classes," she says, "and experience fitness, fun and a deep sense of peace."

2608 West Broadway | Vancouver, BC | V6K 2G3 | **Studios:** 604.739.2009
Lifestyle Store: 604.739.1958 | **Email:** info@semperviva.com | **www.sempervivayogavancouver.com**

L-R: Shera Street, Chidakash

Serenity By The Sea Retreat

Chidakash, Visionary, Counsellor, Energy and Body Worker, Author | Shera Street, Artist, Personal Counsellor, Reiki Practitioner, Psychic, Energy Healer

When guests visit Serenity by the Sea Retreat, an enchanting waterfront retreat located on Galiano Island in the spectacular Gulf Island archipelago, they find themselves on a journey of self-discovery with owners Chidakash and Shera Street. "It is a blessing for us every time we witness the empowerment and vitality that glows in someone who has found his or her way home again to their own special gifts and life purpose," says Chidakash.

Guests can also enjoy healing services under Street's intuitive guidance, including yoga, meditation, creative self-discovery sessions and Expansive Body Integration, an original form of energy bodywork developed at Serenity. "We honour the preciousness of the individual, and deliver our services at the level and pace best suited to the needs and expectations of our clients," says Street.

They were motivated to create Serenity by the Sea Retreat after being 'guided' to an inspiring piece of property where they believed Nature would enhance their healing work. They took different paths in developing their own gifts and spiritual consciousness. Chidakash acknowledges his spiritual teacher: "The years I spent with Osho Bhagwan Rajneesh brought the world of self-empowerment and the sacred to the center of my life." As for Street, a transformational experience "led to Reiki and Gestalt and a new vision of the world—of how people could be together and heal each other—that underlies all the work I do at Serenity."

In keeping with their vision of awakening global consciousness one person at a time, the pair also offers transformational journeys to Machu Picchu and Bali, which "deliver the essential elements of our work—creative self-discovery, spirit, positive intention, and service all experienced in a place of great natural beauty."

225 Serenity Lane | RR2 Galiano Island 42 - 14, BC | V0N 1P0
Tel: 800.944.2655 | Fax: 250.539.2655 | Email: serenity@serenitybythesea.com
Email: serenity@transformationaltours.com | www.serenitybythesea.com | www.transformationaltours.com

Sergio De La Garza

Natural Healing and Bodywork Practitioner

Inspired by many wise teachers who have influenced his life, Sergio De La Garza is a bodywork practitioner who gives from the heart without expectations. Using therapeutic massage, acupressure, Reiki, ear candling and Bach Flower Remedies, among others, he helps his clients take control of their emotions, mind, body and soul so that they can heal and regain balance.

After mastering his own health challenges in his early 20s, De La Garza dedicated himself to healing so that he could share with others what he had learned for himself. "I took control of my life by listening to my inner voice, practising meditation and using a combination of alternative medicine and natural foods to get well," he says.

Currently studying Traditional Chinese Medicine, De La Garza constantly expands his knowledge and services to make his approach as holistic as possible. Through therapeutic massage, he facilitates mental and physical relaxation, as well as increased circulation, mobility and detoxification. With Reiki, healing energy is gently dispersed through his hands, flowing naturally into deficient areas and assisting the body in re-regulating its own energy. Using the Bach Flower Remedies, De La Garza helps his clients resolve emotional or physical disturbances such as insomnia, low self-esteem, depression, anger, sadness or fear, treating the psyche rather than the physical symptoms. Less well-known is Tuina, which resembles a blend of physiotherapy and chiropractics, most effective for soft-tissue injuries, digestive and reproductive disorders, pediatric problems and the treatment of pain. Ear candling, acupressure, reflexology, magnetic cupping massage and Thai stem herb massage complete the impressive menu of modalities.

Yet De La Garza's philosophy is nonetheless simple. "The most important thing about the work I do is helping people get in touch with themselves." he says. "This creates positive energy that stimulates positive changes in people's lives."

404 – 3161 West 4th Avenue | Vancouver, BC | V6K 1R6 | Tel: 604.736.5433
Email: sergio@sergiodelagarza.com | www.sergiodelagarza.com

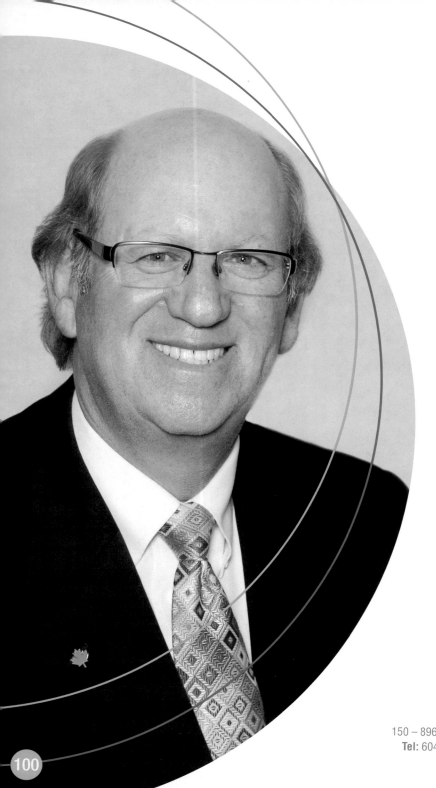

SFU Community Trust/UniverCity

Michael Geller
President and CEO

UniverCity is a vibrant new self-sustaining community that is destined to become an international showcase for innovative and creative approaches to sustainable planning and urban development. Located beside the Simon Fraser University Burnaby Mountain Campus, this community will be known for its well-planned neighbourhoods, strong links to the university and deep respect for the natural heritage of Burnaby Mountain. Its driving force is Michael Geller, SFU Community Trust President and CEO: "Our community is founded on the four cornerstones of sustainability, which guide our work. They include a respect for the environment, a concern for social equity and fiscal responsibility, and a focus on education."

Residents of the new community will enjoy the natural environment provided by 567 hectares of park and conservation area—one of the largest urban forests in the Greater Vancouver area. Forty-five hundred homes will be built over the next two decades with development guidelines ensuring healthier, more energy- and resource-efficient homes designed to suit the mountain's unique climate. An extensive network of pedestrian and bicycle pathways will link the community with the campus and conservation area, and a variety of parks, playfields and public spaces will allow families to meet, play and enjoy community life. Residents will also have access to the Vancity community transit pass, which offers discounted transit throughout the region. UniverCity will be a financially secure community, with a focus on lifelong learning, providing childcare programs, elementary schools and the opportunities afforded by a major university next door.

"Over the next five years, we want to see UniverCity achieve national and international acclaim as an exemplary sustainable community development," says Geller. "In so doing, we hope to inspire other universities and property developers to do the same." Those who choose to live, work or study in the UniverCity community will share a unique lifestyle that offers unparalleled access to a rich diversity of intellectual, social, cultural and recreational resources.

150 – 8960 University High Street | Burnaby, BC | V5A 4Y6 | **Contact:** Nancy McCuaig
Tel: 604.291.3138 | **Fax:** 604.291.3189 | **Email:** geller@sfu.ca | **www.univercity.ca**

100

Shared Vision Magazine

Rebecca Ephraim
Publisher and Co-Owner

Rebecca Ephraim's favourite line is, "You don't have to own a Greenpeace rubber raft to show that you care." And Ephraim, publisher of *Shared Vision* magazine, means it. "You may recycle and I may drive a fuel-efficient car. That may be all we do," she muses. "And that's a beautiful thing 'cause we're doing something!"

She views her monthly publication as a dialogue for change. "I think of *Shared Vision* as a 'coming out' party every month for all the extraordinary people, products and services that are leading the way to a new future," she says. "We connect them with our fabulous —and mostly female—readership." The magazine is a unique blend of engaging and well-researched stories, compelling images and an unparalleled advertising resource that readers use as a trusted guide for making better choices to care for the planet and themselves.

Ephraim is a self-confessed "recovering" TV and radio news anchor and reporter who left the news grind of cataloging the day's horrors. As a media pioneer, she not only nurtures a lighter footprint on the planet but also is passionate in her belief that all of us can contribute. Her suggestions include:

- Whether you're acting as an individual or a business owner, don't be hard on yourself for not doing everything.
- Honour and celebrate the little steps you've taken in your business or personal life that benefit you and your family, your community, and the planet.
- Practice being still in order to rise above the noise. It's fascinating what you'll discover about yourself.
- Support independent media every opportunity you get.

Shared Vision boasts more than 168,000 readers in the Lower Mainland where it's available for free at more than 725 distribution points—from street boxes and coffee shops to "every conceivable" food outlet, as well as online at www.shared-vision.com.

301 – 873 Beatty Street | Vancouver, BC | V6B 2M6 | **Tel:** 604.733.5062
Fax: 604.731.1050 | **Email:** rebecca@shared-vision.com | **www.shared-vision.com**

Clockwise from top: Linda Bakker, Anita Norman, Jami Bennett, Eric Lorenz, Paul Richard

Sierra Club of BC

One Earth. One Chance.

One of BC's best known and most effective conservation organizations, the Sierra Club of BC has played a leading role in environmental stewardship in the province since 1969. Beginning as a small grassroots group of British Columbians dedicated to protecting the spectacular forests and lakes of BC, these early activists joined forces with the U.S. Sierra Club before becoming the first Sierra Club affiliate in Canada. Now known for its innovative communication tools, progressive education programs and positive socio-political impact, the Sierra Club of BC is dedicated to promoting responsible use of the earth's ecosystems and resources.

The Sierra Club's success lies in advocating science-based policy, supporting solid grassroots initiatives and inspiring passionate commitment to the values of environmental stewardship. "We see ourselves as the educators and advocates for urban-related issues, such as climate change and pollution, while still campaigning for the preservation of our wild spaces, parks and natural habitat," says Executive Director Kathryn Molloy. The organization plays a key role in empowering Canadians to not only make personal change but also demand change from their politicians and decision-makers. Each year, its award-winning environmental education program is introduced to 10,000 British Columbian children, teaching them about endangered species, forests, habitat, climate change and pollution.

Working with eight key programs, the Sierra Club focuses on protecting forests and marine ecosystems, promoting new energy solutions and widespread environmental education, organizing guided nature tours, generating state-of-the art maps, developing programs for sustainable communities, and serving as a grassroots hub that enables members and supporters to get involved in meaningful ways.

"One earth, one chance," says Molloy. "We believe in the power of everyone to take action and our goal is to generate that empowerment in engaging and credible ways throughout BC."

302 – 733 Johnson Street | Victoria, BC | V8W 3C7 | **Tel:** 250.386.5255
Fax: 250.386.4453 | **Email:** info@sierraclub.bc.ca | **www.sierraclub.ca/bc**

Simon Says Consulting

Simon Goland
Founder and Alchemist

A self-dubbed "contemporary alchemist," Simon Goland is an educator and facilitator of transformational learning for organizations and individuals. Through his company, Simon Says Consulting, he offers unique programs in professional and personal development that foster lifelong learning and growth. "The capacity to adapt to changing times and circumstances is a lifelong learning process that is crucial to our success as individuals, communities and organizations," says Goland, who has over nine years of experience in developing and delivering lifelong learning programs, workshops and seminars.

Lifelong learning is a multidimensional process that encompasses mental, emotional, physical and spiritual perspectives. Whether that process involves increased self-awareness, enhanced team collaboration or realigned organizational vision, it enables one to continuously evolve and grow. With a focus on sustainable business practices and non-traditional solutions, Goland facilitates this process using diverse ancient and modern approaches and frameworks. Working with numerous local and international organizations, he engages the social capital of organizations—the trust, mutual understanding and shared values and behaviours that bind the members of human networks and foster cooperation.

"Interaction is what enables people to commit to each other and to knit the social fabric of their environments, organizations and communities," says Goland. An engaging, creative educator, he cultivates environments for collaboration and learning, helping his clients develop the clarity and vision they need to define and fulfill their purpose. "Such an inquiry is a wonderful travelling companion both for an individual and for an organization. It sharpens your eye for the road" says Goland. Now in his fourth career, Goland has had his own lessons to learn—letting go of money, status and materialism in order to follow the call of the heart and the needs of the world. A creative visionary and strategist who loves to challenge the status-quo, he embraces the human interpretation of alchemy—the deeper, spiritual transformation of self.

Tel: 604.737.1591 | **Email:** alchemist@simongoland.com | **www.simongoland.com**

Sindy Taylor

Clairvoyant, Intuitive Healer, Reiki Master

"Self-healing is all about empowering ourselves to take control of our health," says clairvoyant, healer and Reiki Master Sindy Taylor. She is speaking from personal experience, having had to make some tough life choices. Refusing conventional Western medicine, she embarked on an alternative healing path that transformed her life. Now, her passion is to bring awareness of the power of self-healing to the global community.

Through her channeled meditations and visualizations, Taylor helps individuals access the healer within and vanquish their fears so that they can fulfil their desires. Working in person or long distance, she also helps people open up to and deal with their psychic abilities, showing them how to apply the principles of self-healing and manifestation. It is through the power of intention, visualization, doing and believing, she says, that individuals can bring about transformation. "Part of my vision is to see children being taught to develop their intuitive abilities in schools," says Taylor. "When they learn how to create and heal from within and to make decisions from the heart versus the mind, they know that all things are possible."

The Wisdom Tree 'art therapy for the soul' is a unique method Taylor uses to aid her clients with their health and well-being using art techniques. Each is a masterpiece she creates while assisting her clients in finding the solutions to their problems. The Wisdom Tree is a true piece of art that can adorn any home, bringing the soul essence of their being into their surroundings. It is a constant reminder of the things one must master in order to attain true health and well-being. "I believe that we surround and adorn ourselves with items of beauty because they bring out the wellness in us, although we may not be aware of it," says Taylor.

3746 West 15th Avenue | Vancouver, BC | V6R 2Z8 | Tel: 604.224.7737
Cell: 604.785.2737 | Email: sintaylor@shaw.ca | www.spiritualhealingarts.com

Skindulgence, The Urban Retreat Ltd

Tazeem Jamal
Spa Director

A feast for the senses, Skindulgence is an elite day spa that blends sophistication with tranquility. With its aromatic scents and plush, earthy décor, the spa transports you to a world of pampering and professional treatments designed to combine results with relaxation. "Our key values are passion, people and professionalism," says spa director Tazeem Jamal, who has been passionately serving the spa's clients for 18 years. The spa's holistic approach to skincare and well-being incorporates non-invasive anti-aging procedures as well as customized treatments and home-care programs.

With an international reputation for excellence, Skindulgence is committed to using the very latest in innovative skincare technology, providing healthy alternatives to highly invasive restorative and cosmetic surgery. It offers over 25 unique and customized facial treatments, using award-winning European skincare lines. "Serious skincare is a non-negotiable necessity," says Jamal. "The skin is the body's largest organ and is constantly exposed to the elements; it needs to be nourished daily."

Other services include exotic exfoliation treatments, make-up artistry, treatments for men, aromatherapy and hot stone massage, an aroma steam shower, laser treatments and some uniquely BC anti-oxidizing treatments—such as organic seaweed and BC glacial clay treatments, and Okanagan wine massages, using real wine extracts. Couples can enjoy a treatment together, with adjoining treatment rooms providing complete privacy and a tranquil escape from the outside world. The spa also provides complimentary beverages and Belgian chocolates, luxurious bath robes and slippers for your personal use, and cozy heated blankets.

Skindulgence believes in nourishing the community too and supports many local charities, including the Breast Cancer Foundation and a women's safe house. "As a local business, we feel it is our privilege and responsibility to give back to the community," says Jamal. So going to the spa is not just good for you; it helps others too.

254A Newport Drive | Port Moody, BC | V3H 5B9 | **Tel:** 604.469.2688
Fax: 604.461.7359 | **Email:** skindulgence@hotmail.com | **www.skindulgencespa.com**

Small Potatoes Urban Delivery Inc. (SPUD)

David Van Seters
President and CEO

SPUD is an innovative grocery-delivery service designed to bring healthy, wholesome food to the doorstep. Catering to busy urbanites who prefer not to spend their free time shopping, SPUD fills an important niche in today's hectic world, helping to reduce waste and promote healthier lifestyle choices. The brainchild of environmental sustainability expert David Van Seters, SPUD was born in 1997 with the purpose of integrating economic, environmental and social values. "At SPUD, we believe that small is beautiful," says Van Seters. "When you buy from us, you make a difference to your community and the environment because we bring you local, organic, wholesome, fairly traded and recycled products. We believe that access to healthy, wholesome food, ethical products and a clean environment is a basic human right."

SPUD is also a compelling example of corporate social responsibility in business. It builds customer relationships that extend beyond product purchases to include dialogue and information exchange. SPUD provides meaningful work, fair compensation, profit-sharing, a spirit of teamwork and opportunities for growth for its staff. It also actively participates in local communities to address food security, human health and well-being, environmental stewardship and economic self-reliance.

"One of the most important factors that cause people to excel is feeling that they are making a difference in the world—that they are contributing to something larger than themselves," says Van Seters. As one of the many pioneers who make BC a leader in sustainability, he is always looking to the future. He sees SPUD expanding to other North American cities so that people begin to associate food delivery with a healthier, more eco-friendly, community-supportive way to buy groceries. In each location, SPUD hires locally, buys locally and supports local community initiatives, making it one of the most socially responsible, environmentally sound and financially viable home-delivery companies in North America.

1660 East Hastings Street | Vancouver, BC | V5L 1S6 | **Tel:** 604.215.7783 | **Cell:** 604.841.6730
Fax: 604.215.1264 | **Email:** david@spud.ca | www.spud.ca | www.spud.com

Sooke Harbour House
Hotel Restaurant Gallery

Frederique Philip
Co-owner and Creative Director

Art and beauty surround guests at Sooke Harbour House—from the delicious food and wine served every day in the restaurant, and the local art that graces each unique room, to the intimate experience of nature just outside. Sooke Harbour House is a memorable setting for refreshing holidays or brief, romantic getaways at any time of year. "No [visit] in my life has been more lovely, contemplative and spiritually rewarding…we will return often and with delight," wrote guest J. M. Shoreline of Washington State. This is the universal experience at Sooke Harbour House.

Guests enjoy exquisite, unique guestrooms and often tour the kitchen garden where over 400 varieties of fresh flowers, herbs and vegetables flourish. In the internationally renowned restaurant, the menu offers only seasonal, local, organic ingredients, including incredibly fresh seafood—all of which is generally served the very day it is caught by local fishers. "For me, buying local food is the only way to support a healthy community," says Frederique Philip, co-owner and creative director. "You have a direct contact with suppliers and customers and using local suppliers does not generate the pollution or waste the energy that buying imported does." This commitment to the local economy is part of the dedication to sustainable business practices that has been in place at Sooke Harbour House since it was founded 27 years ago. "We have always tried to put back as much as or more than we use," says Philip.

During their stay, guests can also enjoy spa services including massage/body or esthetic treatments from the team of trained and certified aromatherapy specialists who carefully prepare herbal essential oils.

1528 Whiffen Spit Road | Sooke, BC | V0S 1N0 | **Tel:** 250.642.3421 | **Cell:** 250.893.3421
Fax: 250.642.6988 | **Email:** frederique@sookeharbourhouse.com | **www.sookeharbourhouse.com**

Soul*ar Energy Holistic Health Enterprises

Laurie Johansen, BScN, Founder, Holistic Nurse, Reiki Master/Educator, Energy and Gemstone Consultant

A car accident in 1992 ended Laurie Johansen's decade-long career as a critical care nurse. She realized some years later that the event was a divine intervention intended to place her firmly on her spiritual healing path. She has spent the past 14 years studying numerous methods of energy-based healing such as Reiki, Neuro-Linguistic Programming (NLP), colour therapy and aromatherapy, in addition to crystals and gemstones, in her search for options to relieve health challenges.

In 1995, she founded Soul*ar Energy Holistic Health Enterprises and, with her business partner, Laurie Ross, eventually began designing energy products from crystals, gemstones and essential oils. These products come with information about their energetic properties and are available for purchase on her website and from local retailers. In addition, Johansen custom-designs pieces for her clients. "Collaborating and co-creating a special healing piece with a client is one of the most rewarding things that I do," she says.

Through designing different products and working with a variety of clients, she has come to understand that energy is the foundation upon which everything is connected. She believes "our mental, emotional, physical and spiritual energetic hygiene is as important as bathing and eating if we are to maintain our well-being and develop an ability to heal ourselves, our planet and each other."

Soul*ar Energy offers online courses including Introduction to Gemstone Jewelry, Working with Gemstones & Crystals, Reiki Levels I & II, and a comprehensive course about energy and coping in today's world, which covers everything from geopathic stress and emotional toxicity, to the vital energy in the foods we eat. With gentle encouragement from the divine, Johansen has committed to share the tools that she has learned. "My healing journey and experience as a clairsentient have taught me a great deal about the world of energy and just how strongly it can affect our lives and sense of well-being."

210 9th Avenue | New Westminster, BC | V3L 2A1 | **Tel:** 604.523.6520
Fax: 604.523.6519 | **Email:** ljohansen@soularenergy.com | **www.soularenergy.com**

Stephen Whipp Team at Berkshire Securities Inc.

Stephen Whipp, Certified Financial Planner, specializing in Ethical Investing

"Many of us jeopardize our retirement and long-term well-being when our investments become divorced from our values," says Stephen Whipp, a Certified Financial Planner with Berkshire Securities Inc. "Failing to invest in ethically or socially responsible ways actually increases our investment risk while diminishing our long-term returns." Committed to values-based investing and financial planning, Whipp helps his clients build wealth while making a positive difference in their financial lives and their community.

As a founding member of the Victoria Values-based Business Network, an organization for entrepreneurs who support sustainability, it is not difficult to see why Whipp's mantra is all about putting your money where your values are. "For companies and our communities to be sustainable, investors must give the same weight to issues such as corporate behaviour, the environment and human rights as they do to profits," says Whipp. He offers ethical portfolio analysis and a variety of investment products, such as ethically managed mutual funds, stocks and bonds, in the context of five core values: professional and personal integrity; strong client relationship; social responsibility; conservative investment philosophy; and transparency in all business dealings.

"Client relationships are the heart of our business and we ensure that they are always founded on mutual respect, trust and shared values," says Whipp, who believes in ethical investing that supports and promotes sound environmental, labour and social practices. Sound long-term financial planning should be about giving back to our local and global communities, he asserts, as well as growing our personal wealth. He also maintains that everyone can build and protect long-term wealth—by following strategies based on buying and holding top-quality, ethically operated businesses. But many individuals often need help and coaching to make their dreams a reality. "We find the right mix of assets for you, so you can sleep at night," says Whipp. "You can create wealth and still satisfy your soul."

202 – 2005 Broad Street | Victoria, BC | V8W 2A1 | **Tel:** 250.405.3550 or 1.866.405.1988
Cell: 250.812.8778 | **Fax:** 250.386.3550 | **Email:** swhipp@berkshire.ca | **www.stephenwhipp.com**

The Stillpoint Center for the Healing Arts

Michelle Benjamin, Co-Founder, Originator of The Osteopathic Field of Awareness Training

At The Stillpoint Center for the Healing Arts, co-founder Michelle Benjamin offers an unusual alternative to traditional medicine, education and spirituality: Parrot Parties. The Parrot Parties stem from Benjamin's study of Osteopathy. Both the US Federal Government and the American Medical Association recognize the Diplomate in Osteopathy as equivalent to a medical degree. Osteopathic practitioners, one of the fastest-growing health professions in the world, treat the whole person, not just symptoms, emphasizing the body's ability to heal itself. Benjamin has applied this knowledge both to the rehabilitation of her animals and to the creation of what she refers to as Parrot Party "atmospheres", whereby she introduces her birds to groups of people interested in learning about their relationship to living, through their interactions with animals.

Benjamin's practice is directed at problems she believes come from the challenge of living a human life in a mechanical society. According to renowned author Joseph Campbell, "The goal of life is to make your heartbeat match the beat of the universe, to match your nature with Nature." Benjamin believes Campbell's wisdom applies to her work. Parrot Parties encourage people to heal in relation to animals, and "animal wisdom is nature personified".

Benjamin adds to her Osteopathic learning experiences, that include movement, sound, music and play to enhance conscious interaction, sometimes in groups of people and sometimes with traumatized animals. The results have consistently helped reintroduce people to their basic, natural human outlook—an outlook that helps them tune in to the world around them, and remind them of their faculty to experience ordinary magic. This helps ease conflict and open opportunities for positive change.

A series of Benjamin's mixed media paintings are on exhibit at The Stillpoint Center's Gallery, with all of the proceeds donated to the further development of care and understanding of traumatized animals.

4419 West 10th Avenue | Vancouver, BC | V6R 2H8 | Tel: 604.224.6857 | Email: michelle@itsforthebirds.net
www.stillpointproject.com | www.itsforthebirds.net | www.dogswithoutharm.com

Sue Studios

Susan Chepelsky
Web Designer

Susan Chepelsky is devoted to the creation of effective visual communication design that brings together individuals who are passionately involved in the pursuit of a spiritual life that incorporates holistic practices and alternative medicine. Her devotion was rewarded when she came upon an unaddressed communication need in the world of holistic healers: whereas they were aware of the connections between mind, body and spirit, few were aware of each other. "I discovered that healers were often isolated, separated or unaware of events, each other and sources of supplies—either local or further abroad," she says. To address this disconnect, she provides clients with unique and sophisticated web-design services, and she serves the whole community through her web portal, the Universal Healing Network.

Chepelsky references life's interconnectedness when describing her approach to web design. "There is a resonant energy web that connects us all and my life purpose is to strengthen this connection, individually and globally." She does this by connecting her clients with others and assisting them in following their path and dreams. Her websites have an undeniable presence on multiple levels and are designed to help illuminate the client's vision, image and spirit. New websites begin with in-depth consultation in comprehensible language, followed by careful planning and frank discussion. The result of her work is always pristine, eye-catching design with clear and intuitive navigation.

The Universal Healing Network comprises a directory of practitioners as well as informative articles, current events and news, and it has become a place to share, connect and learn for both healers and consumers involved with holistic living. "We each carry vital pieces of the 'puzzle' of each others' learning, healing, awakening and growing in this earth journey," says Chepelsky. "In many ways we are here to be each other's catalysts, muses, mentors and inspirations."

210 9th Avenue | New Westminster, BC | V3L 2A1 | **Tel:** 604.525.6770
Email: sue@suestudios.com | **www.suestudios.com** | **www.universalhealingnetwork.com**

Summerhill Pyramid Winery

Stephen Cipes
Proprietor, Honorary Member, Global Vision for Peace,
Founder, Soul of the World Foundation

As Canada's largest certified organic vineyard and most visited winery, Summerhill Pyramid Winery is proud to be a leader in the wine and tourism industry. Twenty years ago, proprietor Stephen Cipes moved from the suburbs of New York City, where there are no fish left in Long Island Sound, to the Okanagan Valley. Seeing the pristine valley for the first time, Cipes and his family vowed to do everything in their power to help keep it as natural as it was that very first awe-inspiring day. They have kept their word by using no herbicides, pesticides or chemical fertilizers in the soil to produce their intensely flavoured small grapes. "We won the gold medal in Champagne, France," he beams, "against French Champagne. These grapes are happy; they're flourishing. Our wines are allowing nature to speak for herself."

Cipes goes the extra mile in the aging of his wines. His award-winning wines are cellared in a precision replica of Egypt's Great Pyramid, built with the wisdom of sacred geometry. Countless blind taste tests over the last 16 years on the effect of sacred geometry on liquids has conclusively proven that clarification and enhancement take place. Cipes offers his pyramid sanctuary as a learning tool for young people. As well, he maintains organic gardens for the Veranda Bistro and for herbs that are being grown to produce a new line of non-alcoholic health elixirs.

Cipes is also founder of the Soul of the World Foundation, a non-profit society in BC, which provides a forum for using alternative power sources, natural earth building, perma-culture as well as discussions for world peace. His vision for Canada is a nation that personifies the values that his winery business and foundation are demonstrating. These two models are based on economic viability, environmental sustainability, and love for all peoples. Summerhill 100% BC-certified, organically grown, pyramid-cellared wines are available globally online at www.summerhill.bc.ca.

4870 Chute Lake Road | Kelowna, BC | V1W 4M3 | Tel: 250.764.4345 | Cell: 250.718.1550
Fax: 250.764.2598 | Email: stephen@summerhill.bc.ca | www.summerhill.bc.ca

Teresa Bockhold Design
Heart & Home Design

Teresa Bockhold
Interior Designer, Feng Shui Consultant, Artist

"A home acts as a blueprint for the life we live or, indeed, wish to live," says feng shui expert Teresa Bockhold. "I help clients create an environment that supports every aspect and aspiration of their lives in a profound way." Principles from ancient and contemporary cultures support the notion of an intimate relationship between the heart and mind and the place called home.

"Thoughts create our reality," says Bockhold, "so there is no better place to begin this process than at our own front door." Crossing the threshold brings new opportunities to support or shift personal patterns and conditions. With her clients, Bockhold explains how their home and its contents reflect their innermost feelings and beliefs, limiting or increasing potential for success in all their endeavours. She makes recommendations for short- and long-term adjustments to their physical environment that will have the potential to create a more healthy, meaningful and abundant life. "It's very rewarding to see the changes in my client's lives once they make the mind/body/environment connection. People are instantly motivated to adjust their home or office space to support their personal transformations. Once they start to see results, the real fun begins!" To achieve the best home environment, Bockhold suggests many elements must be synthesized into a harmonious whole. As a fine artist, she recognizes that choosing room colours is an art in itself. Each colour resonates with distinct associations—physical and psychological—affecting mood and function. "Much of my work involves bringing the perfect colour palette to each space, inside and out," she says.

Designing space is a personal journey with universal implications. By making conscious and authentic choices, the spirit flows outward and returns in kind. This is the essence and power of feng shui, a philosophy that is over 3,000 years old and whose wisdom is available to everyone.

Tel: 604.926.3000 | **Email:** tbockhold@telus.net
www.teresabockholddesign.com | www.heartandhomedesign.com

Teresa Hwang Feng Shui & Design

Teresa Min Yee Hwang
Traditional Chinese Feng Shui Consultant,
Interior Designer

Traditional or classical Chinese feng shui has a history of 6,000 years in China. It is comprised of the observation of forms in the environment, detailed calculation of formulas based on time and space, the use of the Luo Pan (Chinese feng shui compass), and the logical study and implementation of the balance and harmony of chi. Originally, feng shui was used to locate the best burial sites, but then the ancients realized the same principles could be applied to the living, and the study of this art evolved to what we know of it today.

Teresa Hwang, feng shui consultant and interior designer, is a student of world-renowned Feng Shui Master Joseph Yu, BSc. Hwang is one of Master Yu's Feng Shui Research Centre Senior Practitioners and Lecturers. She grew up in Hong Kong and became accustomed to the principles of this unique blend of art and science as her father subscribed to the wisdom and practiced it at home. "He was constantly rearranging furniture and moving homes when I was growing up," she says. "I did not realize his purpose until I started studying feng shui myself." Hwang adapts the ancient practice to the modern-day needs of her clients, providing consultations for private homes and businesses, as well as new construction and renovation projects. She also offers classes and other educational opportunities to her clients. "My goal is to educate the public in the true teachings of traditional Chinese feng shui, and in how to improve one's life by incorporating good feng shui and good karma—the major influencing factors in a person's destiny."

Practicing the art of promoting mental, physical and physiological well-being through arranging and designing her clients' home and work environments, Hwang applies the ancient belief in patterns of yin and yang and the flow of chi. "My clients enjoy the benefits of good feng shui in their environment—balance and harmony."

8809 Okanagan Landing Road | Vernon, BC | V1H 1J9 | **Tel:** 250.549.1356 or 604.321.0608
Email: fengshui@teresahwang.com | **www.teresahwang.com**

Tides Canada Foundation

Tim Draimin
Executive Director

Tides Canada Foundation, Canada's first national public foundation focused on the environment and social justice, provides strategic philanthropic services to donors who are passionate about changing the world. The Foundation acts as a bridge, connecting donors with innovative charities targeting the root causes of social and environmental problems in Canada and worldwide. Its services make giving to charity simple, cost-effective and tax-efficient for donors. And because their giving strategies are aligned with their personal values, donors experience greater impact, enjoyment and purpose in their charitable giving.

Innovators throughout the global charitable sector are making a real difference with creative strategies and programs. They may be a small, rural group in the Maritimes or a mid-sized one in downtown Vancouver, but their prescient and practical ideas can spread and build a momentum for positive social and environmental change. To maximize their potential, Tides Canada connects them with donors who think big and give wisely—promoting far-sighted environmental stewardship and progressive social change. The Foundation is fast becoming an innovative leader in promoting Giving and Learning Circles for donors in Canada, while educating donors and the public on strategic charitable giving and social investing.

Tides' Executive Director Tim Draimin encourages everyone to explore the power of giving. "Take stock of the money, time and expertise you can contribute to charitable work and develop a giving strategy," he says. "Determine what you want to see accomplished and look for smart ideas that leverage big outcomes." Many grassroots and community-based organizations have great track records for delivering results and everyone benefits when donors are discerning and strategic in their donations. "Be engaged and proactive with your giving," says Draimin, "because every giving decision you make is an important investment in the future."

680 – 220 Cambie Street | Vancouver, BC | V6B 2M9 | Lesley Anderson, Director of Philanthropic Services
Tel: 604.647.6611 | **Toll-free (Canada and US):** 1.866.TIDESCA (843.3722) | **Fax:** 604.647.6612

360 – 215 Spadina Avenue | Toronto, ON | M5T 2C7 | **Tel:** 416.481.8652 | **Fax:** 416.979.3936
Email: info@tidescanada.org | **www.tidescanada.org**

Tigress Ventures

Angela Reid
President, Politician, Public Speaker, Writer, Community Activist

A passionate visionary, environmental entrepreneur and sustainability advocate, Angela Reid creates and promotes holistic business models that accelerate shifts towards economic, social and environmental sustainability, while furthering social education, action and positive change. She is also a motivational and transformational speaker, raising awareness and helping individuals, businesses and governments to see and understand the positive social, environmental and economic benefits of sustainability.

"Growth has two fundamentally different meanings: expansion—getting bigger, and development—getting better," says Reid. "I help individuals, groups and corporations identify solutions that lead to responsible growth. Internationally, there are many proven examples of effective sustainable practices that are financially successful. We need only adapt, fine-tune and apply these concepts to many of the challenges in our own homes and communities." Reid seeks to extend her innovative models into provincial, state, national and international markets. To this end, her company, Tigress Ventures, has researched and compiled extensive information on alternative energy, green building design, organic agriculture and preventative healthcare—in the context of environmentally and socially responsible business and public policy.

The Tigress Ventures logo is of a triple goddess, with the three figures representing the innocent maiden who sees the world through the eyes of a child, the nurturing and devoted mother, and the wise, intuitive elder. Reid calls upon all of these strengths in her work and believes that many of the solutions to current global challenges are in the hearts and hands of women. Reid is a tigress herself. She has run for political office four times, sits on the councils for both the provincial and federal Green Parties, and is the CEO of her local Green Party organization. She is also a folk singer, songwriter and guitar player whose music moves people to positive social action by creating joy, love and confidence.

PO Box 20103 | Kelowna, BC | V1Y 9H2 | **Tel:** 250.215.7714
Email: angela@tigressventures.ca | **www.tigressventures.ca**

Tum Tum Tree Designs

Stacy Wolfenden
Hemp Clothing Designer and Manufacturer

Motherhood brought more change to Stacy Wolfenden's life than just becoming a parent. With the admonition of Mahatma Gandhi in mind, "Be the change that you wish to see in the world," she founded Tum Tum Tree Designs following the birth of her first child, creating children's clothing in the highly green product of hemp fibre. "Having my children made me realize that I needed to do something more meaningful," she says. "I wanted to do something that looks further than just the next generation."

Tum Tum Tree Designs creates clothing and accessories in classic styles to serve several generations of children. The outstanding design innovation at Tum Tum Tree is that many products are reversible, yielding two items for the price of one. Longevity and durability of Tum Tum Tree products are assured by the use of hemp—hemp being up to four times stronger than cotton and naturally resistant to pests, mold and mildew. As well, the hollow-core fibre of hemp makes it an excellent insulator offering ideal protection against ultraviolet radiation.

Wolfenden's interest in hemp extends beyond its practical value. As with many individuals living in the natural splendor of British Columbia, she has a passionate commitment to the environment. By choosing to use hemp at Tum Tum Tree, she supports the cultivation of a natural product that requires less water to grow, has a higher yield than most other fibres and requires no chemicals for cultivation. "Do all that you possibly can to reduce your ecological footprint now," she says to other entrepreneurs thinking of starting their own businesses.

"Make a statement about your values and ideals with your dollars," she says. "Supporting local businesses makes economic sense—the less we rely on others, the better off our communities will be." Shopping with Tum Tum Tree Designs means supporting more than a local business—it is a vote in favour of localized sustainable business and environmental practices.

L-R: Sydney, Ty, Stacy Wolfenden

Tel: 604.676.9897 | **Email:** stacy@tumtumtreedesigns.com | **www.tumtumtreedesigns.com**

117

Vancity

Derek Gent
Investment Manager, Social Enterprises

Integrity, innovation and responsibility—these are the key values that provide the framework for how Vancity Capital Corporation operates. It's a conscious financial institution that not only cares about protecting its investors, but proactively seeks out opportunities in social and environmental causes, as well as contributing to and being part of the Vancouver community. The higher risk venture arm of Vancity Credit Union, Vancity Capital, is set up to finance projects that may not fit all of the conventional-loan or granting criteria of a bank or credit union.

According to investment manager Derek Gent, Vancity is able to do amazing things by using a long-term, sustainable investment lens, and taking a venture capital approach to social change and ecological sustainability. "Our role is to work with individuals and groups to realize their aspirations and visions—whether it's an eco-lumber cooperative seeking funding to increase its sales volumes, or a not-for-profit property management venture requiring capital to launch housing initiatives that support women and children impacted by violence," says Gent. "Through a dedicated portfolio of social enterprise investments, we strive to enhance capacity within non-profit and cooperative organizations in BC, and to invest in initiatives that achieve significant social, environmental and financial results."

Vancity has supported a wide range of enterprises and community organizations through creative solutions that help define potential opportunities that exist between philanthropy and financial markets. They are able to take members' capital and put it to the best use possible to achieve a range of goals and maximize the returns—whether financial, social, cultural, or ecological—on multiple bottom lines. "We have evolved from pioneering efforts in corporate social responsibility to broader and more ambitious work in sustainability, accountability and, more recently, community leadership," says Gent. "At Vancity, we are hoping to change the world and make things better, while always honouring and remembering where we came from and why we exist."

PO Box 2120, Station Terminal | Vancouver, BC | V6B 5R8
Tel: 1.888.826.2489 | Email: derek_gent@vancity.com | www.vancity.com

Vancouver Waldorf School

Education Towards Freedom

The Vancouver Waldorf School is part of the world's largest independent school movement—a movement founded in 1919 by the renowned Austrian philosopher, educator and scientist, Rudolf Steiner. After the horrors of World War I, Steiner committed himself to creating a pedagogy focused on nurturing "free-thinking individuals unfettered by dogma, fear or coercion"—an education system that would create a population capable of bringing peace and prosperity to the world. A Waldorf education fosters in children a sense of reverence and respect for all life; it creates a worldview in which innovation is measured by the good it brings many rather than the short-term gain it may offer a few.

The Waldorf curriculum recognizes the need for human beings to develop intellectually, emotionally and spiritually, giving each student a strong academic foundation enriched by the fine arts and applied skills. It focuses on the present—what the child needs to learn now—in contrast with mainstream education's emphasis on enabling the choice of a future career path. Ask a Waldorf student, "What do you want to be when you grow up?", and you will get the response: "I don't need to wait 'to be.' I am what I choose to be right now."

The school addresses and enriches each individual's aptitudes by utilizing the developmental tasks that define each stage of human development. Further, while the uniqueness of each student is valued, learning is always a group activity, which encourages the development of a profound social consciousness and respect for others—an integral part of this artistically and academically stimulating environment. Waldorf students do not just simply adapt to the demands of a quickly changing economic environment—they do so with the conviction that their personal success must contribute to a greater good and to social renewal.

2725 St. Christophers Road | North Vancouver, BC | V7K 2B6
Tel: 604.985.7435 x 202 | **Fax:** 604.985.4948 | **Email:** rgill@vws.ca | **www.vws.ca**

Clockwise L-R: Konrad Lasocki, Pele Phair, Emma Powers, Silvia Formankova

119

vancouveryoga.com

Eoin Finn, Founder, Yoga Teacher, 'Blissologist'
Insiya Rasiwala, Yoga Teacher, 'Bliss Promoter,' Writer

Some people just go straight to the core of things—like Eoin Finn. The founder of vancouveryoga.com, Finn promotes the experience of bliss—through his yoga classes, workshops, philosophy debates, retreats and his fearless, effervescent nature. With fellow yoga teacher and writer Insiya Rasiwala, Finn also helps to educate and inspire those seeking to balance their personal desires with the well-being of others.

"Yoga is such a powerful metaphor in our lives today," says Finn. "It enables us to continually consider and connect to our world— to see that all life is interconnected and that our individual actions have collective repercussions."

Influenced by the teachings of Joseph Campbell, Finn got off the business treadmill and made a commitment to only do things that deeply inspired him. He forged a philosophy of fearlessness, believing that things work out if he manifests what is deep in his heart. Rasiwala made a similar life shift, abandoning the world of corporate advertising and marketing in favour of a lifestyle yielding more intangible yet positive benefits. She now applies the legacy and philosophies of her Indian homeland—yoga, Ayurveda and the teachings of Gandhi—to help others find their bliss.

Both teachers are active volunteers in their community, with Finn serving as co-visionary and 'yogi-in-chief' for the Annual Camp Moomba Yogathon and teaching yoga at St Paul's Hospital, and Rasiwala teaching yoga to kids in the public schools and providing yoga outreach services. Through their online portal, they also promote sustainable businesses and services, offer free yoga MP3 downloads, sell their own yoga DVDs, organize Yoga Ecology and Surf (YES) retreats and offer workshops throughout North America. And for those feeling a little low on the 'blissometre', Finn recommends a spoonful of honey—for its sweet essence and the fact that it represents the entire ecosystem to which we are all connected.

151 – 1917 West 4th Avenue | Vancouver, BC | V6J 1M7
Tel: 604.732.3108 | Email: info@vancouveryoga.com | www.vancouveryoga.com

WarriorSage

Satyen Raja
Master Trainer and Facilitator

Satyen Raja, founder and president of WarriorSage, is a living synthesis of Eastern wisdom and Western practicality, combining the power of the warrior and the wisdom of the sage. Raja is one of the very few lead facilitators of the Zen-based Illumination Intensive, and the first to make this technique available on an international scale. This course, along with his Sex, Passion & Enlightenment Intensive, are two of a range of courses he has taught to thousands of students internationally.

Raja teaches with clarity, power and provocation. In his presence, his students are compelled to search within and to draw out their latent abilities. Through dynamic examples, compelling stories, cutting-edge ideas, spontaneous humour and proven practices, Raja motivates, provokes and inspires students to surrender to their own greatness. When he teaches, he holds nothing back; he gives his students all of himself.

"I use my gifts to take you to magical realms and to deeply feel into your closures," he says. "I bring your fears and your unconscious, self-limiting patterns to the surface." Combining his intuition with experience, Raja ripens students by exposing their deepest heart. He sees his students at their core and takes them past their edge to where real transformation takes place.

The path of the WarriorSage is not necessarily the gentlest path of spiritual growth. It is, however, fast. This level of spiritual practice is intense; students must be willing to go into the fire with him. "I offer opportunity for transformation out of my deep love for those with whom I work, indeed, for everyone," he says. Raja is the teacher only for those who are seeking real change.

PO Box 12033, Murrayville RPO | Langley, BC | V3A 9J5 | **Tel:** 604.534.0616 or 1.800.815.1545
Fax: 604.534.0661 | **Email:** info@warriorsage.com | **www.warriorsage.com**

West Coast Institute of Mystic Arts

Erin Arnott
Owner

The mystic arts are centuries old but still relevant today. The word 'mystic' refers to mysteries transcending ordinary human knowledge. Our society has lost touch with many of the age-old traditions that could benefit us in today's busy world. Erin Arnott is the owner of West Coast Institute of Mystic Arts (WCIMA) in North Vancouver. "Our goal is to empower—to show you how to trust your own intuitive abilities and to help you live your life to the fullest," she says. "We help you find your path to bliss and teach you how to harness the power of your authentic self."

WCIMA is the modern-day version of what the ancient Greeks called a mystery school. Its curriculum includes: the intuitive arts and psychic development; the healing arts and personal growth; the art of science (sacred geometry, astrology); ancient ceremony from all cultures; respect and connection with the earth from all backgrounds; and prayer from all religions. The Institute educates and teaches metaphysical certification courses such as astrology, meditation, vibrational healing, all levels of Reiki, electromagnetic field balancing, feng shui, massage, Ortho-Bionomy® and reflexology. It also offers workshops and lectures given by some of today's top practitioners in their field.

Arnott's vision is to help heal the world one person at a time. "I have learned to love life, live with gratitude and happiness, and to simply let life unfold," she says. As a result, WCIMA provides a safe space, a knowledgeable faculty and diverse programming, while encouraging students to discover the knowledge, wisdom, and ability to know their true essence and power.

102 – 88 Lonsdale Avenue | North Vancouver, BC | V7M 2E6
Tel: 604.982.0099 | Email: info@mysticarts.ca | www.mysticarts.ca

Whole Dyslexic Society

Sue Hall
Founder

Some of the smartest people can't read, but that doesn't mean they are less intelligent. There are those who think in words and those who think in pictures—with the latter being more curious, creative and intuitive, and highly aware of their environment. However, since almost all traditional learning environments are geared exclusively towards 'word thinkers', the 'picture thinkers'— dyslexics—are left to struggle through the best they can. "Ideally, there would be a perfect balance between the two worlds," says Sue Hall of the Whole Dyslexic Society (WDS). "We would all acknowledge that different is okay and we would all learn the way we were born to learn. Dyslexics are not 'learning-disabled'. It is the lack of awareness and understanding of their particular learning style that inhibits their learning."

The WDS creates a safe learning environment for participants to interact and experience success. Created by a dedicated team of volunteers, the organization addresses the needs of dyslexics, their families and their community, in an environment of accelerated learning that promotes healing, understanding and support for individual growth and development. "Every individual loves learning if their unique learning style is honoured," says Hall. "We encourage the current education system to become more aware of this dynamic."

Through their diverse programs, bursaries and a new, unique, full-time learning centre, the WDS enables individuals to discover their talents, resolve individual challenges and realize that learning really can—and should—be fun! It addresses the cause of the so-called learning challenges, so that the symptoms fall away. "The 'gift' of dyslexia cannot and should not be cured," says Hall. "It needs to be understood and facilitated so that innate talents can flourish. Our goal is to provide the tools for enhancing self-esteem and self-worth, enabling individuals to fulfill their potential."

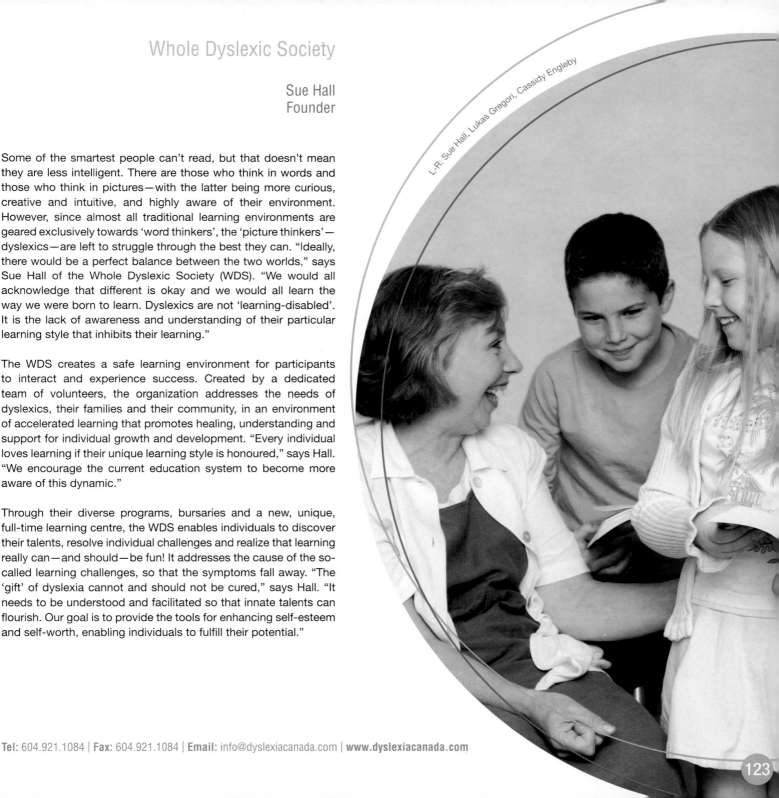

L-R: Sue Hall, Lukas Gregori, Cassidy Engleby

Tel: 604.921.1084 | **Fax:** 604.921.1084 | **Email:** info@dyslexiacanada.com | **www.dyslexiacanada.com**

Wholistically Speaking

Sharon Richlark, BA, BEd
Homeopath, Biotherapeutic Drainage/Bio-Resonance/
Certified Auricular Therapist, Medical Intuitive

A health and wellness consultant with over 20 years of specialized training and experience, Sharon Richlark works with clients from all over the world. Her ambition is to educate, support and inspire people to create emotional, physical and spiritual balance in their lives. Richlark has a unique and multifaceted background. Trained first as an educator, she later became a Homeopath and an ordained Minister and hosted a radio program called *Wholistically Speaking* that showcased a variety of topics on health and wellness. She is also a medical intuitive who has studied advanced healing techniques with leading natural healers, Auricular therapists and doctors of Homeopathy and Traditional Chinese Medicine, enabling her to use a variety of tools and approaches in her private practice.

Richlark specializes in identifying the blockages and imbalances that create today's countless diseases. Using Bio-Resonance Therapy—a system for strengthening the body's natural electromagnetic oscillations while cancelling pathological oscillations—as well as Biotherapeutic Drainage Therapy, which involves detoxifying the body using complex homeopathic remedies, Richlark addresses numerous conditions. Through personal health evaluations and detailed client profiles, she screens for viruses, bacteria, parasites, fungus, heavy metals and chemicals; redresses physical, emotional and spiritual imbalances; and provides individualized treatment programs for candida, allergies, chronic/acute conditions, auto-immune disorders, ADD/ADHD and post-traumatic stress—using specialized European homeopathics, botanicals and supplements.

Many of Richlark's clients have reached the end of the medical line when they come to see her, seeking answers that traditional healing modalities could not provide. With her understanding of the stressors that create physical and emotional pain, plus her willingness to explore every avenue to provide balance for her clients, she helps them remove the blockages to health and to achieve positive, tangible results. "There is no disease except congestion," she says, "and no cure but circulation."

Tel: 604.990.8926 or 1.866.867.3771 | **Email:** wholisticallyspeaking@telus.net
www.wholisticallyspeaking.com | www.therapeuticreadings.com

Wisdom Is Within Coaching

Liz Robitaille
Life Coach, Author, Mentor,
Workshop Facilitator, Louise L. Hay Teacher

Offering knowledge and skills that foster love, self-acceptance, compassion and abundance, Liz Robitaille empowers people to live their best life and recognize their potential for love and success. Her extensive training has led to her certification as a Louise L. Hay teacher. Through her business, Wisdom Is Within Coaching, Robitaille has enhanced the lives of hundreds of people with her workshops, personal coaching, keynote addresses and writing. "Learning to love and accept ourselves and others frees us from expectations and opens doors to greater happiness and trust," she says. "Relationships improve, self-esteem emerges and our world is richer on all levels."

Robitaille offers one-and two-day workshops on topics such as dissolving emotional blocks, how to love yourself, inner child issues, body wisdom and prosperity. Her 12-month Self-Discovery Works program is designed for individuals who are ready to take their life to a higher level of prosperity, with participants creating personal goals and objectives to move into the next stage of their lives. Her teacher-training program offers coaches and healers mentoring on business building and training to complement and empower their personal vision. She offers personal-coaching services, phone consultations, monthly affirmations and teleconferences via her website.

Supporting others in taking back their power and becoming the stewards of their lives is Robitaille's passion. Working with the belief that every individual makes a difference when they fully develop themselves, she helps people release the old stories that keep them stuck in recurring cycles. "I believe we are motivated by our need for love and approval," she says. "When we can appreciate our journey without self-criticism or judgement, we awaken to a new level of love and acceptance. And as we heal ourselves, we help heal our world."

Tel: 250.757.9794 or 604.960.0625 | **Email:** liz@wisdomiswithin.com | **www.wisdomiswithin.com**

Worldview Strategies

Jessie Sutherland
Conflict Transformation Specialist,
Teacher, Writer, Life Coach

With 20 years of experience as an educator in cross-cultural communication, community development, international affairs and conflict resolution, Jessie Sutherland helps her clients expand awareness of self, others and the environment, while increasing their effectiveness in the face of personal, community and global changes. With a particular commitment to improving cross-cultural relations, she works extensively on building the relationship between First Nations and non-Aboriginal people. Her published work on reconciliation has, according to Chief Robert Joseph, Hereditary Chief of the Gwa Gwa Enuk First Nations, "the potential to provide the spark to bring real peace, balance and harmony between parties, and between Canada and its Aboriginal people."

Inspired by her work in northern indigenous communities, Mali and Peru, Sutherland spent several years researching the nature of collective denial and how to shift collective consciousness to move out of our current era of increased human conflict and environmental devastation. Now, through her company, Worldview Strategies, she offers an innovative approach to transforming relationships and empowering individuals, organizations and communities to become their own agents for change.

She has taught a wide spectrum of people working on complex reconciliation issues—from government leaders and members of grassroots national organizations, to faith communities and youth groups. "My passion lies in inspiring others and promoting the spontaneous insights and revelations that lead to personal transformation and societal change," says Sutherland. The full scope of her worldview work is best understood through her highly praised book, *Worldview Skills: Transforming Conflict from the Inside Out.*

In partnership with Simon Fraser University's Dialogue Programs, Sutherland is launching an exciting cross-cultural and multisectoral community dialogue series called *Finding Home: Belonging, Connection and Community*. Sutherland also offers workshops, teleconferences, courses and public speaking—helping others become instruments of transformation in their own communities.

PO Box 74606 | 2768 West Broadway | Vancouver, BC | V6K 2G4 | **Tel:** 604.879.2402
Email: jessie@worldviewstrategies.com | **www.worldviewstrategies.com**

Yoga West / Raj Yog Nivas

Home of Kundalini Yoga, Vancouver

A leader in its field for over 30 years, Yoga West specializes in Kundalini yoga—an ancient blend of breath, movement, meditation and mantra, designed to expand awareness and boost health and vitality. It increases oxygen capacity, boosts blood flow, balances the glandular system, strengthens the nervous system and reduces stress. Kundalini yoga comes from an Indian lineage thousands of years old and was brought to the West in the late 1960s by Yogi Bhajan who was declared a Master at the age of 16. It is a powerful modern-day system for dealing with the challenges and stresses of everyday life. It brings practitioners a heightened self-awareness and vitality that allows them to harness mental and emotional energy, feel more steady and stable, have enhanced peace of mind and concentration, and gain a deep inner calm.

"No matter what we achieve, our successes are hollow unless we fulfill the soul's yearning to bring higher consciousness into our daily lives," says Dharm Kaur Khalsa, longtime Yoga West teacher. Kundalini yoga allows the self to wake up to its true nature. It is contained within a form of yoga called Raj yoga—the yoga of majestic presence—which taps into the healing force of love that is constantly unfolding in life. Kundalini yoga awakens you to the experience of this unfolding using powerful kriyas (sets of exercises), pranayam (breath), mantra and meditation.

Yoga West offers daily Kundalini yoga classes, weekend workshops and a daily sadhana (early morning yoga and meditation) for strong, disciplined practice. Through its sponsor, Raj Yog Nivas, it also offers men's and women's camps, Kundalini Yoga Teacher Training, Conscious Pregnancy Training, Sat Nam Rasayan practice sessions, White Tantric Yoga and Sikh-related programs. Yoga West is a service offered by Raj Yog Nivas that is sponsored by the 3HO Foundation—an international non-profit society established in 1969 by the Master of Kundalini Yoga, Yogi Bhajan.

L-R, Back Row: Guru Kirn Kaur Khalsa, Suckbinder Kaur Bains, Dharm Kaur Khalsa, Bir Kaur Khalsa, Hari Bhajan Singh Khalsa

L-R, Front Row: Hari Singh Khalsa, Guru Raj Kaur Khalsa

2662 West 4th Avenue | Vancouver, BC | V6K 1P7 | **Tel:** 604.732.YOGA (9642)
Email: info@yogawest.ca | www.yogawest.ca | www.khalsaladiescamp.com | www.khalsamen.com

YWCA of Vancouver

Janet Austin
CEO

The YWCA of Vancouver is a registered charity that touches the lives of over 43,000 individuals and families each year. This special organization provides resources for women, their families and those seeking improvement in the quality of their lives. Offering programs dealing with affordable housing, child care, leadership, wellness and innovative employment training, the YWCA is integral to the well-being of the community.

CEO Janet Austin is the first to admit that her work with the YWCA is incredibly rewarding. "Our vision is of a world where no one need go hungry or homeless, where women live safely and free from violence, where children get the best start in life, and young people face life's challenges, healthy in mind, body and spirit," says Austin. "The YWCA is a place where the poorest families in our society, single moms and their children, have access to child care and housing services that help lift them out of poverty."

The YWCA of Vancouver isn't just involved, it leads the way: the YWCA believes, for example, that a universal child-care system will lead to healthy children and a strong economy. The organization and its 400 volunteers know that creating a healthy society requires an integrated vision that links our social and physical environments. They are committed to innovation that supports sustainability in order to create better futures for children, youth and women. Austin knows it's a huge vision, but the right vision and the YWCA invites the community to help translate that vision into reality. Says Austin, "The impact that the YWCA can have on social policy and creating a healthy society is amazing and truly powerful, and the positive changes we see in people's lives is inspiring."

Program Centre, 535 Hornby Street | Vancouver, BC | V6C 2E8 | Tel: 604.895.5800
Fax: 604.684.9171 | Email: enquire@ywcavan.org | www.ywcavan.org

Zentrepreneurism

Allen Holender
Speaker, Author, Broadcaster, Zen Mentor

Zentrepreneurism is based on a profound, but practical, philosophy that builds upon capitalism's strengths, combined with a higher purpose—one that is an inspiring new value system for business leaders. Allan Holender is one of those leaders, integrating his personal vision with his professional mission. Every day, zentrepreneurs are adding new enterprises to the spectrum of successful, purposeful organizations following a new and better model for doing business. Holender observes that work alone isn't enough for many individuals today. "People are looking for 'a whole life experience,' a life where our partners, our families, our companies and our efforts merge into a single, harmonious whole—where we measure our success in more ways than just the balance in our bank accounts."

Joel Bakan, author and screenwriter of *The Corporation* asserts "Allan reveals the valueless and destructive tendencies of contemporary business...while remaining passionately and optimistically committed to the possibility of a better future."

As a leadership and teambuilding trainer, Holender has developed programs for universities, hospitals and corporations. He has mentored entrepreneurs, CEOs and senior management from some of North America's top-ranked companies. He is also a popular media personality and commentator in Canada and the United States. In his recent book, *Zentrepreneurism: A 21st Century Guide to the New World of Business*, Holender states, "While an entrepreneur creates a business, a zentrepreneur creates a business and a life." The book, currently available at book stores and through his website, www.zentrepreneurism.com, studies an enlightened brand of capitalism that fuses service to others with a fresh perspective of entrepreneurial spirit. Anyone interested in zentrepreneurism can join a like-minded community through the site, where individuals can connect, collaborate, exchange ideas and stories, mastermind, and learn more from each other about ethical capitalism.

102 – 2101 McMullen Avenue | Vancouver, BC | V6L 3B4 | **Tel:** 604.684.9224
Cell: 604.312.7661 | **Email:** allanholender@shaw.ca | **www.zentrepreneurism.com**

"We are failing to provide the freedom of future generations to sustain their lives on this planet."
– MILLENNIUM REPORT OF THE SECRETARY-GENERAL OF THE UNITED NATIONS

ADDITIONAL
RESOURCES

SOCIAL ACTIVISM, COMMUNITY-BUILDING AND CONSCIENTIOUS COMMERCE

"Never doubt that a small group of thoughtful, committed citizens can change the world. Indeed, it's the only thing that ever has."
– MARGARET MEAD

Take action!

01. Align your investments with your personal values
02. Ask questions, do the research, and make informed choices
03. Be integral with your word
04. Be the change you want to see in the world
05. Become intentional – discover your personal purpose and live it
06. Buy local, organic, fair trade, second-hand, eco-friendly
07. Create community in any way you can
08. Demand full disclosure on food labels
09. Don't confuse money with wealth
10. Eat at an Ocean Wise restaurant or marketplace and choose seafood items that are labelled as sustainable
11. Educate yourself about your consumer choices
12. Engage with decision-makers and call on them for leadership to protect more forests, protect endangered species habitat, ban toxic chemicals and create aggressive strategies to reduce global climate change
13. Gain media literacy so that you can see through the news stories presented by large corporate media
14. Join a co-op
15. Look for fair trade and union labels
16. Pass on all the smartest things you know to the most promising youth who will listen to you
17. Run for office
18. Support climate-friendly politicians
19. Support public transportation
20. Support the Kyoto Protocol
21. Support the non-profit organizations, causes and charities you believe in
22. Understand how your actions have a global impact
23. Vote
24. Vote with your dollar
25. Write to your elected officials, participate in rallies and support environmental organizations

Books recommended by our contributors

01. *Affluenza*, by John de Graaf, David Wann, Thomas H. Naylor
02. *Cradle to Cradle: Remaking the Way We Make Things*, by William McDonough, Michael Braungart
03. *Fast Food Nation: The Dark Side of the All-American Meal*, by Eric Schlosser
04. *Global Profit and Global Justice: Using Your Money to Change the World*, by Deb Abbey
05. *How Much Is Enough? The Consumer Society and the Future of the Earth*, by Alan Durning
06. *Integral Psychology: Consciousness, Spirit, Psychology, Therapy*, by Ken Wilber
07. *Marketing that Matters: 10 Practices to Profit Your Business and Change the World*, by Chip Conley and Eric Friedenwald-Fishman
08. *No Logo: No Space, No Choice, No Jobs*, by Naomi Klein
09. *Reclaiming Higher Ground: Creating Organizations that Inspire the Soul*, by Lance Secretan
10. *Rich Dad, Poor Dad*, by Robert Kiyosaki
11. *Secrets of the Millionaire Mind: Mastering the Inner Game of Wealth*, by T. Harv Eker
12. *Slow is Beautiful: New Visions of Community, Leisure and Joie de Vivre*, by Cecile Andrews
13. *The Cultural Creatives: How 50 Million People are Changing the World*, by Paul H. Ray and Sherry Ruth Anderson
14. *The Ecology of Commerce*, by Paul Hawken
15. *The Tipping Point*, by Malcolm Gladwell
16. *The Troublemaker's Teaparty: A Manual for Effective Citizen Action*, by Charles Dobson
17. *Unnatural Law: Rethinking Canadian Environmental Law and Policy*, by David R. Boyd
18. *Values-Shift: The New Work Ethic and What it Means for Business*, by Dr John Izzo
19. *What Matters Most: How a Small Group of Pioneers Is Teaching Social Responsibility to Big Business, and Why Big Business Is Listening*, by Jeffrey Hollender
20. *Workers of the World Relax*, by Conrad Schmidt

ENVIRONMENT AND SUSTAINABILITY

> "Nobody made a greater mistake than he who did nothing because he could do only a little."
> — EDMUND BURKE

Take action!

01. Buy a hybrid or more fuel efficient car
02. Buy things that last
03. Carry a refillable water bottle
04. Carry a reusable bag for shopping
05. Choose energy-efficient lighting and appliances
06. Compost
07. Conserve energy in every way you can
08. Conserve hot water
09. Consume less, waste less
10. Eat less meat
11. Get a home energy audit
12. Heat and cool your house efficiently
13. Install solar panels
14. Install compact fluorescent light bulbs
15. Insulate your house
16. Limit paper use and buy tree-free or post-consumer recycled paper
17. Purchase carbon-offset credits to neutralize carbon emissions
18. Reduce air travel
19. Replace your toilet with a low-flush model
20. Reuse before you recycle
21. Switch to green power
22. Turn off the tap when you brush your teeth
23. Use a clothesline instead of a dryer
24. Use alternative fuels
25. Walk, bike, ride transit, car pool

Books recommended by our contributors

01. *An Agricultural Testament*, by Sir Albert Howard
02. *An Inconvenient Truth*, by Al Gore
03. *At the Cutting Edge*, by Elizabeth May
04. *Dead Reckoning: Confronting the Crisis in Pacific Fisheries*, by Terry Glavin
05. *Ecological Literacy*, edited by Michael Stone and Zenobia Barlow
06. *Global Marine Biological Diversity: A Strategy for Building Conservation into Decision Making*, by The Center for Marine Conservation
07. *Greenhouse: The 200-Year Story of Global Warming*, by Gale E. Christianson
08. *Greenpeace: The Inside Story*, by Rex Weyler
09. *It's Easy Being Green: A Handbook for Earth-Friendly Living*, by Crissy Trask
10. *Last Frontier Forests: Ecosystems and Economies on the Edge*, by Dirk Bryant, Daniel Nielsen and Laura Tangley
11. *Lock Me Up or Let Me Go: The Protests, Arrest and Trial of an Environmental Activist*, by Betty Shiver Krawczyk
12. *Marine and Coastal Ecosystems & Human Well-being: Synthesis*, United Nations Millennium Ecosystem Assessment Board
13. *Marine Life of the Pacific Northwest: A Photographic Encyclopedia of Invertebrates, Seaweeds and Selected Fishes*, by Andy Lamb & Bernard Hanby
14. *Sacred Balance: Rediscovering Our Place in Nature*, by David Suzuki with Amanda McConnell
15. *Sea Change: A Message of the Oceans*, by Sylvia Earle
16. *Seeds of Deception*, by Jeffrey M. Smith
17. *Stolen Seeds: The Privatization of Canada's Agricultural Biodiversity*, by Devlin Kuyek
18. *Stormy Weather: 101 Solutions to Global Climate Change*, by Guy Dauncey
19. *Superbia! 31 Ways to Create Sustainable Neighborhoods*, by Dan Chiras and Dave Wan
20. *The Weather Makers: How Man Is Changing the Climate and What it Means for Life on Earth*, by Tim Flannery

HOLISTIC HEALTH AND WELLNESS

"The doctor of the future will give no medicine, but will interest the patient in the care of the human frame, in diet and in the cause and prevention of disease."
—THOMAS A. EDISON

Take action!

01.	Act from your heart
02.	Ask your healthcare practitioner which herbal supplements, vitamins and minerals would be most beneficial for you
03.	Attune with Mother Nature every day
04.	Be authentic, grateful and kind to all living systems
05.	Be responsible for your health, your thoughts and your actions
06.	Believe in yourself
07.	Bless your food and water before ingesting
08.	Breathe deeply
09.	Celebrate the small things
10.	Do what you love
11.	Drink more water
12.	Eat less saturated fat and processed foods, and more whole grains, complex carbohydrates, fruits and vegetables
13.	Eat wholesome, organic food
14.	Establish a support team, group, a coach—anything to support positive growth
15.	Exercise and eat well to keep your body, mind and spirit strong
16.	Grow a garden
17.	If you are faced with an illness, thoroughly research and explore it on all levels—emotional, physical, mental, spiritual and environmental—to try to eliminate the possible root causes
18.	Keep learning and pushing the boundary of your capacities
19.	Know yourself
20.	Meditate. Love. Serve.
21.	Move your body
22.	Practice love, respect, tolerance, sharing and forgiveness
23.	Practice preventative medicine and try an alternative modality
24.	Trust your inner voice and intuition
25.	Try a yoga class

Books recommended by our contributors

01.	*Ageless Body, Timeless Mind* and *The Seven Spiritual Laws of Success*, by Deepak Chopra
02.	*Anatomy of the Spirit: The Seven Stages of Power & Healing*, by Caroline Myss
03.	*Blue Truth, The Way of the Superior Man* and *Dear Lover*, by David Deida
04.	*Bountiful Beautiful Blissful: Experience the Natural Power of Pregnancy and Birth with Kundalini Yoga and Meditation*, by Gurmukh Kaur Khalsa
05.	*Child Honouring: How to Turn This World Around*, edited by Raffi Cavoukian and Sharna Olfman
06.	*DreamHealer 2, Guide to Self-Empowerment*, by 'Adam'
07.	*Emotional Intelligence: Why it Can Matter More than IQ*, by Daniel Goleman
08.	*Healthy Aging, The Healthy Kitchen, 8 Weeks to Optimum Health*, and *Spontaneous Healing*, by Dr Andrew Weil
09.	*Light on Life*, by B.K.S. Iyengar
10.	*Prescription for Nutritional Healing: A Practical A-to-Z Reference to Drug-Free Remedies*, by Phyllis A. Balch
11.	*Spiritual Nutrition*, by Gabrielle Cousens
12.	*The Art of Happiness: A Handbook for Living*, by Dalai Lama, Howard C. Cutler
13.	*The Artist's Way*, by Julia Cameron
14.	*The Four Agreements: A Practical Guide to Personal Freedom*, by Don Miguel Ruiz
15.	*The Hidden Messages in Water*, by Masaru Emoto
16.	*The Power of Intention*, by Dr Wayne W. Dyer
17.	*The Power of Myth*, by Joseph Campbell
18.	*The Power of Now: A Guide to Spiritual Enlightenment*, by Eckart Tolle
19.	*Women's Bodies, Women's Wisdom*, by Dr Christiane Northrup
20.	*You Can Heal Your Life*, by Louise Hay

CONTRIBUTORS' RECOMMENDED MOVIES & WEBSITES

"Never discourage anyone who continually
makes progress, no matter how slow."
— PLATO

Movies

01. *1 Giant Leap* | www.1giantleap.tv
02. *Affluenza* | www.pbs.org/kcts/affluenza/map/map.html
03. *An Inconvenient Truth* | www.climatecrisis.net
04. *Blue Vinyl* | www.bullfrogfilms.com/catalog/bv.html
05. *Born Into Brothels* | www.kids-with-cameras.org
06. *Bowling for Columbine* | www.bowlingforcolumbine.com
07. *The Boys of Baraka* | www.theboysofbaraka.com
08. *The Corporation* | www.thecorporation.com
09. *Deconstructing Supper*
    www.bullfrogfilms.com/catalog/decon.html
10. *End of Suburbia* | www.endofsuburbia.com
11. *Fahrenheit 911* | www.fahrenheit911.com
12. *The Future of Food* | www.thefutureoffood.com
13. *Ghandi*
14. *The Great Warming* | www.thegreatwarming.com
15. *Indigo* | www.indigothemovie.com
16. *Microcosmos*
17. *One* | www.onetheproject.com
18. *Passionate Harvest* | espresso101.com/books_dvds/dvds/666
19. *Scared Sacred* | www.scaredsacred.org
20. *The Secret* | www.thesecret.tv
21. *Super Size Me* | www.supersizeme.com
22. *The True Cost of Food*
    truecostoffood.com/truecostoffood/movie.asp
23. *What the Bleep Do We Know?* | www.whatthebleep.com
24. *What Babies Want* | www.whatbabieswant.com
25. *Who Killed the Electric Car?*
    www.sonyclassics.com/whokilledtheelectriccar

Websites

Health and Wellness:

01. American Holistic Medical Association | www.holisticmedicine.org
02. CAMline | www.camline.org
03. Canadian Health Network | www.canadian-health-network.ca
04. Deepak Chopra | www.chopra.com
05. Dr. Andrew Weil | www.drweil.com
06. DreamHealer | www.dreamhealer.com
07. Go Gratitude | www.gogratitude.com
08. Healthworld Online | www.healthy.net
09. HealthWWWeb | www.healthwwweb.com
10. Yoga Journal | www.yogajournal.com

Environment and Sustainability:

01. An Inconvenient Truth | www.climatecrisis.net
02. BC Sustainable Energy Association | www.bcsea.org
03. David Suzuki Foundation | www.davidsuzuki.org/Take_Action
04. Earth Future | www.earthfuture.com
05. Light House: Sustainable Building Centre |
    www.sustainablebuildingcentre.com
06. Markets Initiative | www.marketsinitiative.org
07. Organic Trade Association | www.ota.com
08. Planet Friendly | www.planetfriendly.net
09. The Climate Trust | www.climatetrust.org
10. TransFair Canada | www.transfair.ca

Social Activism, Community Building and Conscientious Commerce:

01. Bioneers | www.bioneers.org
02. Business Alliance for Local Living Economies | www.ballebc.com
03. Canadian Business for Social Responsibility | www.cbsr.bc.ca
04. Code Pink | www.codepink4peace.org
05. Co-op America | www.coopamerica.org
06. Social Venture Network | www.svn.org
07. The Canadian Centre for Policy Alternatives | www.policyalternatives.ca
08. The Tyee | www.thetyee.ca
09. Utne Magazine | www.utne.com
10. Victoria Values Based Business Network | www.vbnetwork.ca

CONTRIBUTORS' RESOURCES

> "The reward of a thing well done is to have done it."
> —RALPH WALDO EMERSON

Books and Publications

01. *Aromatherapy Tool Kit: Blending by Condition*, by Pamela Stroud
02. *Back in Control - Back Injury Prevention Workbook and Manual*, by Barbara Purdy
03. *Fit for Love – find your self and your perfect mate*, by Olga Sheean
04. *Get Me Out of Here - Emergency Evacuation Training Manual*, by Barbara Purdy
05. *Heart of a Woman*, by Sheryl Roush with writings from Jan Mills
06. *Hollyhock Cooks*, by Linda Solomon and Moreka Jolar
07. *Inner Expression*, by Shera Street
08. *Journeys to Wellness: A Workbook to Discover Personal Paths to Wholeness*, by Marilyn Hamilton, BC CGA PhD, with Barry Stevenson, MSc MSc (HSP)
09. *Keeper of the Dreams*, by Shera Street and Amrit Chidakash
10. *Sierra Life Monthly*, by The Sierra Club of BC
11. *Sierra Report Quarterly*, by The Sierra Club of BC
12. *Soul Spa™, 7 essential life practices for building joy, balance and fulfillment developed specifically for women*, by Linda-Ann Bowling
13. *The Business of Kindness…creating work environments where people grow*, by Olivia McIvor
14. *Worldview Skills: Transforming Conflict from the Inside Out*, by Jessie Sutherland
15. *Zentrepreneurism*, by Allan Holender
16. *30 Ways of Getting More Out of Travelling - Anywhere!* by Amrit Chidakash

Multimedia

Music and Guided Meditations:

01. *Angels in the Amrit: A Live Chanting Recording*, by Madeleine Bachan Kaur
02. *Breathe Through: A Guided Rebirthing Experience*, by Mahara Brenna
03. *Caring for our Coast: Living Oceans Society Compilation of Artists*
04. *Chakras: Pathways to Well-being*, by Ilona Hedi Granik
05. *Collective Creativity Instructional CD for Teachers*, by Angela Roy
06. *Finding New Life…On the Other Side of Grief and Loss*, by Mahara Brenna
07. *Inner Being: Meditations Within the Elemental Kingdoms*, by Ilona Hedi Granik
08. *Managing Stress: Stress Management and Meditation/Visualization Techniques*, by Jan Mills
09. *Next Move*, by Rae Armour
10. *Solar Morning Lunar Evening, Visualization Meditations*, by Mahara Brenna
11. *Soul Songs: Sacred Music Album for Meditation, Relaxation and Inspiration*, by Madeleine Bachan Kaur
12. *The Tambour Moving Arts Project Children's World Music*, co-recorded by Angela Roy

Instructional DVDs:

01. *Advanced Yoga Flow for Strength and Flexibility*, by Janis Goad
02. *Back to Basics: Patient Handling Transferring Techniques*, by Barbara Purdy
03. *Foot Reflexology: A Step-by-Step Guide*, by Chris Shirley
04. *Gentle Yoga For Seniors and Beginners*, by Janis Goad
05. *Get Me Out of Here! Emergency Evacuation Training*, by Barbara Purdy
06. *Journey on the Mat*, by Emmie Li
07. *Yoga for Advanced Beginners and Intermediates*, by Janis Goad
08. *Yoga for an Advancing Practice*, by Janis Goad

Short Films:

01. *Bali-Journey and Journals*, by Shera Street
02. *Birds in the City 2002*, by Madeleine Bachan Kaur
03. *Hiking the Inca Trail to Machu Picchu*, by Amrit Chidakash
04. *Sound of Life- Life of Sound 2006*, by Madeleine Bachan Kaur

GLOSSARY

Acupuncture: A therapeutic technique that originated in China more than 5,000 years ago. Tiny needles are inserted along the body's meridians (or energy channels) to stimulate the vital energy, or qi, that must flow unobstructed throughout the body in order for health to be maintained. When this energy is blocked or becomes stagnated, illness and disease result.

Alternative Medicine: Any therapy that is not considered mainstream. These therapies, by definition, are used instead of conventional or western medicine and tend to be holistic, focusing on all aspects of the individual.

Aromatherapy & Essential Oils: The use of essential oils (extracts or essences) from flowers, herbs and trees to promote health and well-being. These oils can be applied directly to the body or used in atomizers.

Astrology: The art and science of clarifying the fundamental themes of a person's life in accordance with the aspects of the planets, moon and sun in the 12 Zodiac positions at the moment of one's birth.

Ayurveda: An ancient Hindu medical-metaphysical healing science based on harmonizing body and mind through diet, exercise, herbs and purification procedures. It recognizes four distinct constitutional types, each requiring different regimens and lifestyles in order for good health to be maintained. Focusing on self-healing using natural remedies, it seeks to heal the fragmentation and disorder of the mind-body complex to restore wholeness.

Carbon Offset: When you fly, drive or heat your home, your carbon dioxide emissions add to global warming. A carbon-offset program or credit enables you to offset these emissions through the funding of sustainable-energy projects.

Chakra: A Sanskrit word meaning 'wheel' or 'circle'; usually refers to the body's seven main energy centres located along the spinal column and in the brain, each of which has an emotional and spiritual function. If one or more chakras are out of balance, physical, emotional or mental disease can result. Keeping chakras aligned and clear can enhance one's well-being, sense of purpose and emotional stability.

Channelling: Transmission of information or energy from a nonphysical source through a human 'channel' or 'medium' who is often in a trance during the communication.

Chelation Therapy: A treatment for certain types of heavy-metal poisoning or toxicity; it pulls heavy metals and toxins from the body and has been used to treat cancer.

Chiropractic: The main focus of chiropractic is the relationship between the skeleton (particularly the spine) and the nervous system. Misalignments of the vertebrae caused by poor posture or trauma can lead to decreased function, pain and illness. The chiropractor uses his or her hands to manipulate the spine and bring it back into alignment. Chiropractic is commonly used to treat back pain, headaches and injuries. It is also used as a preventative therapy.

Clairvoyance: The paranormal ability to see psychic information, including historical or future events or other phenomena that cannot be discerned naturally through the five material senses. Also called ESP.

Colour Therapy: A form of therapy based on the principle that colour has a profound effect on the physical, mental, emotional and spiritual aspects of the self. When applied to light, food and clothing, colour therapy is considered to have wide-ranging curative effects and is often used to balance and enhance the body's energy.

Complementary Medicine: Generally refers to the use of an alternative medicine in conjunction with conventional or Western treatment.

Conservation: Literally means 'protection against undesirable changes' and usually refers to the sustainable use of organisms or ecosystems so that biodiversity and the natural environment are preserved.

Corporate Social Responsibility: Generally refers to an on-going commitment by businesses to behave ethically and to contribute to economic development while demonstrating respect for people, communities, society and the environment. It unites the concepts of global citizenship, environmental stewardship and sustainable development.

Craniosacral Therapy: A hands-on treatment for pain and loss of function due to restrictions in the craniosacral system, which includes the brain, spinal cord, skull bones, sacrum (base of spine) and the fluid and membranes around these structures. Practitioners apply gentle pressure and make adjustments, primarily to the cranium.

Cultural Creatives: A term coined by sociologist Paul H. Ray and psychologist Sherry Ruth Anderson to describe a large segment of Western society that is weaving a new cultural fabric, reframing how we see the world today. These activists—schoolteachers, artists, spiritual guides and scientists—are questioning the unspoken assumptions of the old culture, opening up new insights and forging creativity in people's lives from the grassroots levels. There is growing evidence that these efforts are changing society in many positive ways.

Doula: From the ancient Greek word for a woman who personally serves another woman. The word has come to mean a woman experienced in childbirth, who provides continuous physical, emotional and informational support to the mother before, during and just after childbirth. She ensures that the mother and family understand the benefits, risks and alternatives relating to all tests and procedures so that any unnecessary interventions, medication or Caesarian sections are avoided.

Eco-Efficiency: Minimal ecological impact based on the idea of doing more with less. According to the World Business Council for Sustainable Development, it means making production processes more efficient and creating more goods and services with fewer resources and less waste and pollution.

Ecology: The study of the distribution and abundance of living organisms and how such distribution and abundance are affected by interactions between the organisms and their environment. The term 'eco-friendly' is often used to describe actions that are friendly to natural environments.

Electro-Pollution: The harmful levels of electromagnetic fields that are emitted by all electrical appliances, cell phones and transmission lines. These fields can have an adverse effect on human health, including a range of conditions, from headaches and flu-like symptoms, to chronic fatigue and depression. In extreme cases, they can cause leukemia and tumours.

Energy Alternatives: See Renewable Energy

Energy Healing: A general term for modalities that are based on the idea that the human body consists of energy fields that can be stimulated through various techniques in order to promote wellness. The concept of vital energy can be traced back to the oldest medical systems and is known as qi in China, ki in Japan, and prana in India. The underlying principle of energy healing is that a strong flow of vital energy is the key to maintaining health. A practitioner working with vital energy seeks

GLOSSARY

to help the patient rebalance his or her energy in the body, by stimulating, unblocking or dispersing it. The result is enhanced well-being.

Environmental Conservation: The rational use and protection of the environment to ensure that humans and the natural world can co-exist sustainably.

Ethical Consumerism: Buying things that are made in ethically and eco-friendly ways. Generally, this means without harm to, or exploitation of, humans, animals or the natural environment. Consumers can promote positive buying by favouring ethically produced products, or negative purchasing by boycotting a particular product or company.

Fair Trade: A trading partnership, based on dialogue, transparency and respect, that promotes greater equity in international trade. It contributes to sustainable development by offering better trading conditions to, and securing the rights of, marginalized producers and workers, especially in the South. Fair trade organizations (backed by consumers) are actively engaged in supporting producers, awareness-raising and campaigning for changes in the rules and practices of conventional international trade.

Feng Shui: The ancient Chinese art of placement. It involves balancing, healing and enhancing energies by integrating people, buildings and landscape to achieve harmony with nature. The goal is to optimize the flow of qi, the vital life force of the universe, to promote good health, positive relationships, prosperity, career growth, happiness and more. Practitioners assist their clients in creating a healthy personal and home environment.

Forest Stewardship Council: The only forest certification system broadly endorsed by environmental and social organizations internationally. FSC is an independent, third party certification scheme that audits 'on-the-ground' logging operations according to 10 international principles and criteria designed to ensure sustainable logging operations.

Global Warming: The gradual heating up of the globe as a result of solar heat being trapped in the atmosphere by a build-up of carbon dioxide and other gases. The burning of fossil fuels (such as coal, gas and oil) and the clearing of forests have dramatically increased the amount of carbon dioxide in the Earth's atmosphere, causing a rise in temperatures, melting of the polar ice caps, and extreme weather phenomena that affect wildlife and human habitats.

GMO or GE: Acronyms for 'genetically modified organisms' and 'genetically engineered', respectively. Both mean the same thing: that the genetic code in the DNA of an organism has been altered by either inserting, removing, damaging or shifting the natural gene sequences and composition, through means other than cross-breeding, cross-pollination, fermentation, hybridization, in-vitro fertilization or tissue culture.

Green Living: A lifestyle that actively promotes and embraces social justice, a healthy community and ecological balance.

Greenhouse Gases: Gaseous components of the atmosphere that contribute to the greenhouse effect (global warming). Some greenhouse gases occur naturally in the atmosphere, while others result from human activities.

Hawaiian Lomi Lomi: An ancient healing form of massage from Hawaii that works the muscles with continuous, flowing strokes, encouraging the recipient to relax, let go and simply be.

Health: A state of complete physical, mental and emotional well-being and not merely the absence of disease.

Herbal Medicine: See Western Herbal Medicine

Holistic Health: A state of well-being and wholeness that comes from integrating and working with all aspects of the human being—physical, emotional, mental and spiritual.

Holistic Medicine: The art and science of healing that addresses the whole person—body, mind and spirit—to promote optimal health. Holistic physicians emphasize personal responsibility and educate their patients about how to take care of themselves at all levels of their being.

Homeopathy: A healing system founded in the 18th century by Samuel Hahnemann, based on three principles: like cures like (Law of Similars); the more diluted the remedy, the stronger or more potent it is (Law of Infinitesimal Dose); and illness is individual and holistic. Homeopathy attempts to stimulate a person's natural healing processes with minute dilutions of natural substances.

Integral Theory: Integral theory refers to the systematic holistic philosophy developed originally by Ken Wilber, and more recently incorporated into the Spiral Dynamics theory developed by Don Beck. Based on the premise that a comprehensive understanding of humans and the universe can be obtained by combining scientific and spiritual insights, it is an all-encompassing evolutionary theory that addresses all aspects of consciousness studies as well as such diverse fields as ecology and politics.

Integrative Medicine: A healing-oriented medicine that takes account of the whole person (mind, body and spirit), as well as lifestyle. It emphasizes the therapeutic relationship and makes use of all appropriate therapies—both conventional and alternative—while encouraging patients to actively participate in their own healthcare through nutritional and lifestyle adjustments and mind-body therapies such as yoga and meditation.

Kinesiology: The study of the anatomy, physiology and mechanics of body movement and muscle function in humans. A kinesiologist's scope of practice is broad and may include the following: assessment of human movement, performance and function; and prevention and management of disorders to maintain, rehabilitate or enhance movement, performance or function in the areas of sport recreation, work and exercise. Practitioners may also provide consulting services, conduct research and develop policies related to rehabilitation, human motor performance, ergonomics and occupational health and safety.

Kinesiology, Applied: A form of diagnosis that uses muscle-testing, developed by chiropractor Dr George Goodheart, as a feedback mechanism for determining how a person's body is functioning. Using muscle-testing, a skilled practitioner can obtain feedback about physical, emotional, mental, spiritual and nutritional factors affecting an individual's health or performance.

Local Living Economy: An economy that provides secure and fulfilling livelihoods for all, working in harmony with natural systems, supporting biological and cultural diversity, and fostering a healthy community.

LOHAS: An acronym for 'lifestyles of health and sustainability'. LOHAS consumers are those who are passionate about the environment, sustainability, social issues and health. They are variously referred to as cultural creatives, conscious consumers

GLOSSARY

or LOHAS consumers, and represent a sizable group in the United States: 17% of adults or 36 million consumers.

Life Coaching: A form of coaching that helps people to effectively deal with personal/professional issues and to accomplish their goals in life. It draws from a number of disciplines, including sociology, psychology and career counselling, and is designed to help unlock people's potential and enable them to move forward.

Massage Therapy: A therapeutic form of massage designed to heal injury, relieve psychological stress, manage pain and improve circulation. Usually applied to soft tissue, muscles, connective tissue, tendons, ligaments, joints and lymphatic vessels to achieve a beneficial response.

Meditation: A technique for centering and focusing the mind to bring about internal stillness, often facilitated by focusing on one's breath, an object or a mantra. Meditation can calm the central nervous system, relieve stress and anxiety, alleviate depression and help the mind open up to guidance from a higher power.

Midwife: A responsible and accountable professional who works in partnership with women to give the necessary support, care and advice during pregnancy, labour and the postpartum period, and to provide care for the newborn. This care includes preventative measures, the promotion of normal birth, the detection of complications in the mother and child, the accessing of medical care or other appropriate assistance, when necessary, and the carrying out of emergency measures, if required.

Natural Medicine: A system of integrated healthcare that incorporates clinical nutrition, herbal medicine, lifestyle counselling, and the use of vitamins, minerals and other nutrients to treat the patient holistically. Natural medicine practitioners treat the underlying cause of disease rather than the symptoms, enabling the patient to heal from within and preventing chronic syndromes from developing.

Naturopathic Medicine (also known as Naturopathy): A branch of medicine that relies on natural remedies to improve health and treat disease by enhancing the body's innate ability to heal itself. Naturopathy takes a holistic approach to health, using a broad array of modalities, including manual therapy, homeopathy, hydrotherapy, herbalism, acupuncture, counselling, environmental medicine, aromatherapy and nutritional supplementation.

Nutritional Counselling: A form of counselling that helps individuals to make positive lifestyle changes in accordance with their specific nutritional needs. Using several approaches, a counsellor can determine the nutrients required to aid digestion, assimilation and metabolism, as well as other herbal therapies and/or exercise programs designed to restore and promote optimum body functioning and performance.

Organic Food: Food produced according to certified organic farming standards, which means crops grown without the use of conventional pesticides, artificial fertilizers or sewage sludge; animals reared without the routine use of antibiotics or growth hormones; and food processed without ionizing radiation or food additives. Organic food is also free of genetically modified organisms.

Organic Certification: A certification process for producers of organic food and other organic agricultural products. In general, any business directly involved in food production can be certified, including seed suppliers, farmers, food processors, retailers and restaurants. Requirements generally involve a set of production standards for growing, storage, processing, packaging and shipping that include the avoidance of synthetic chemical inputs (eg, fertilizer, pesticides, antibiotics, food additives, etc) and genetically modified organisms; the use of farmland that has been free from chemicals for a number of years (often three or more); keeping detailed written production and sales records (audit trail); maintaining strict physical separation of organic products from non-organic products; and undergoing periodic on-site inspections.

Osteopathy: A branch of medicine that originally used strictly manipulative techniques for correcting somatic abnormalities thought to cause disease and inhibit recovery. However, over the past century, osteopathy has embraced the full spectrum of medicine, including the use of prescription drugs and surgery, in addition to manipulative techniques.

Physiotherapy: A form of therapy concerned with the assessment, diagnosis and treatment of disease and disability through physical means, such as massage, exercise, heat or electrotherapy. This includes the restoration of movement, natural breathing etc, after an operation or an accident.

Pilates: A system of exercises developed by Joseph Pilates, a German-born athlete and physical-therapy pioneer, who believed that physical fitness was the first requisite of happiness. He defined physical fitness as, "the attainment and maintenance of a uniformly developed body with a sound mind fully capable of naturally, easily and satisfactorily performing our many and varied daily tasks with spontaneous zest and pleasure" (Pilates, Joseph, Return to Life, 1945).

Post-Consumer Waste: Recovered paper material from products generated by businesses or consumers, which have served their intended end uses and have been separated or diverted from solid waste for the purpose of collection and recycling.

Psychic: The ability to perceive things usually beyond the normal range of perception. A psychic is attuned to subtle faculties and energies, resulting in extra-sensory perception that may take the form of clairvoyance, clairaudience, precognition, psychometry or kinesthetic knowing.

Psychotherapy: Psychological treatment for emotional problems, whereby a qualified therapist helps to remove, modify or reduce existing symptoms, establish healthy patterns of behaviour, and promote positive personality growth and development.

Qigong: A component of Traditional Chinese Medicine that combines movement, meditation and focused breathing to enhance the flow of vital energy (qi) in the body, to improve blood circulation and to enhance immune function.

Rebirthing: A form of conscious breathwork that involves reliving the experience of being born in order to release anxieties believed to result from the original experience. Said to enhance emotional, mental, physical and spiritual well-being while promoting self-awareness.

Recycling: The reprocessing of materials that would otherwise become waste, in order to make new products. Recycling keeps waste out of landfills, prevents waste incineration and reduces consumption of new raw materials and energy.

Reflexology: A form of hands-on therapy designed to stimulate the glands, organs and other parts of the body by working on corresponding reflex points on the hands, feet or ears. By applying pressure to these points, a reflexologist can ease tension, improve circulation and promote the natural function of the related area in the body.

Reiki: An energy healing system based on ancient Tibetan knowledge, discovered by Mikao Usui in Japan in the early 1900s. The word Reiki comes from two Japanese

GLOSSARY

words—Rei and Ki—meaning universal life force energy. This energy is said to be transmitted via the practitioner whose hands can be gently placed on the body or slightly above it to facilitate healing and relaxation for the recipient.

Renewable Energy: Any form of energy that can be captured via existing flows of energy resulting from on-going natural processes, such as sunshine, wind, flowing water, biological processes and geothermal heat flows. Neither fossil fuels nor nuclear power are considered to be renewable.

Shamanism: An ancient spiritual and medical tradition practised in native cultures around the world. Using ritual, shamans often enter altered states of consciousness to promote the healing of their clients. Shamans regard themselves as conductors of healing energy and/or information from the spiritual realm.

Social Entrepreneur: Someone who identifies and applies practical solutions to social problems by combining innovation, resourcefulness and opportunity. He/she operates according to certain social values and is fully accountable to the constituencies that he/she serves. This kind of entrepreneur starts with a vision and a well-thought-out roadmap to ensure the success and sustainability of his/her venture.

Socially Responsible Investing: A style of investing that combines a desire to maximize financial return with an attempt to maximize social good. In general, socially responsible investors favour corporate practices that are environmentally responsible, support workforce diversity, increase product safety and quality, and are founded on sound ethical principles.

Sustainable Community: A sustainable community is one that continually adjusts to meet the social and economic needs of its residents while preserving the environment's ability to support it.

Sustainability: The ability to provide for the needs of the world's current population without damaging the ability of future generations to provide for themselves. When a process is sustainable, it can be carried out over and over without negative environmental effects or prohibitive costs for anyone involved.

Traditional Chinese Medicine: A 3,000-year-old system of holistic medicine combining the use of medicinal herbs, acupuncture, food therapy, massage and therapeutic exercise. Chinese physicians look for the underlying causes of imbalance in the 'yin' and 'yang', which lead to disharmony in the 'qi' or vital energy in the body. With a focus on preventing disease, they identify how illness manifests itself in a patient and then treat the patient, not the ailment or disease itself.

Triple Bottom Line: A business model whereby equal importance is placed upon the social, environmental and financial aspects of the business. This triad-like philosophy considers social progressiveness and environmental excellence to be as important as profitability. This means that we do not maintain systems that use up and discard people (social) or the environment (non-renewable resources) in order to make money.

Vibrational Medicine: A form of medicine that works with the body's energy and is based on the principle that humans are dynamic energy systems. This approach sees health and illness as originating in subtle energy systems, which coordinate the life-force and are affected by emotions, spirituality, and nutritional and environmental factors. Vibrational medicine embraces acupuncture, aromatherapy, Bach Flower Remedies, chakra rebalancing, channelling, colour therapy, crystal healing, absent healing, electro-acupuncture, homeopathy, the laying on of hands, meridian therapy,

moxibustion, past-life regression, Polarity Therapy, psychic healing, psychic surgery, Reiki, toning, transcendental meditation, and Therapeutic Touch, among others.

Visualization: The process of creating and focusing on a mental picture or image, often for the purpose of healing or achieving a particular goal. A guided visualization is one that is facilitated by a third person who talks the individual through their visual journey.

Watsu™: A form of aquatic bodywork involving stretching and Shiatsu, which is applied while being floated in warm water. The water temperature (around 35 °C) promotes deep relaxation. The recipient is continuously supported by the therapist while he or she rocks and gently stretches the body. Because it is performed in the water, the body is free to be manipulated and stretched in ways impossible while on the land. Watsu helps relieve mental stress, increases flexibility, strengthens muscles and aids in injury recovery.

Western Herbal Medicine: A holistic system that combines conventional medicine, herbal remedies, nutrition and lifestyle to restore and stimulate the body's natural ability to heal itself. The treatments take into account the individual's physical, physiological and emotional needs. The use of herbs is based on empirical and scientific knowledge of the medicinal properties of plants and their effects on different body systems. All herbal formulas are individually created and compounded to meet the specific needs of each patient.

Yoga: From the Sanskrit word for union. An ancient Indian philosophy and system of postures, breathing techniques, visualization, relaxation, meditation, diet, cleansing regimes and way of life. There are many different types of yoga that vary slightly in their approach. Yoga is practiced to establish a healthy, lively and balanced approach to life, to achieve self-awareness, and union with the Divine.

Yoga Therapy: A form of therapy and/or instruction that involves yoga postures and teachings to prevent, reduce or alleviate structural, physiological, emotional and spiritual pain, suffering or limitations. Usually conducted in private sessions so as to cater to the specific needs of the individual. Designed to release physical and emotional tension, the therapy may also involve breathing techniques, visualization, cleansing processes and meditation, in addition to the yoga postures.

Zero Waste: A concept that requires us to change our thinking so that nothing is viewed as waste. In a zero-waste society, nothing would be thrown away and everything would be utilized for something. Many perfectly good resources are treated as waste, rather than being re-used, and our world is showing the signs of this mismanagement.

The glossary was compiled with help from the following sources:

www.zerofootprint.net | www. naturespath.com | aims.ubc.ca
www. drcobi.com | www. thepilatesden.com | www. reiki.nu
www. marketsinitiative.org | www. coopamerica.org | cmbc.bc.ca
www. pacificreflexology.com | www. mindbodyhealing.ca
www. fraserbasin.bc.ca | en.wikipedia.org

INDEX

INDEX

CONTENTS

DAY 1

Exodus 1:9-10

*And [the king] said to his people,
"Look, the people of the children of Israel are
more and mightier than we; come,
let us deal wisely with them, lest they multiply,
and it happen, in the event of war, that they
also join our enemies
and fight against us, and so go up
out of the land."*

A Green-ey'd Monster

Shakespeare called it a "green-ey'd monster." The English poet John Dryden called it "the jaundice of the soul." Most of us simply call it jealousy.

Under any name jealousy can have dreadful results. When a Pharaoh "who knew not Joseph" came to power in Egypt, he grew jealous and fearful of Israel's prosperity. Consequently, he enslaved them to ensure they posed no threat to his rule.

When Herod heard from the Magi that a "King of the Jews" had been born, he jealously moved to guard his authority by committing a heinous crime. He ordered all the male babies in the vicinity of Bethlehem slain.

Jealousy in the life of a Christian is equally harmful. Ministries have been ruined, the

4

work of the Spirit squelched and personal testimonies tarnished by a jealous attitude. Many years ago the famous sculptor Michelangelo and the equally famous painter Raphael were commissioned to create works of art for the beautification of the Vatican. Each had a different job to do and both were highly respected, yet there developed such a bitter spirit of rivalry between them that finally they would not even speak to one another when they met. Their jealousy was obvious to all who knew them in spite of the fact that they both were supposedly doing their work "for the glory of God."

Never treat jealousy lightly. Confess it as sin; treat it as sin; forsake it as sin. Then pray for God's blessing on the person or situation that aroused the jealousy. You may be surprised to find the overflow of that blessing filling your own life. Jealousy in your life creates barrenness in your soul. It's time to get rid of the jealousy and enjoy the blessing.

Jealousy does more harm to its owner than its enemy.

Reflections/Prayer Requests

_____

_____

_____

5

DAY 2

Exodus 1:17
But the midwives feared God, and did not do
as the king of Egypt commanded them, but
saved the male children alive.

No Fear

At the funeral of John Knox, the great Scottish reformer, it was said, "Here lies one who feared God so much that he never feared the face of any man." This attitude is often reflected in Scripture. There are at least 116 places in the Bible where we are told to "fear the Lord"—not in a cringing, servile fashion, but in a healthy sense of awe, wonder and reverence. It is the kind of fear that enables us to place the One feared above everything else.

We see this attitude in the lives of two women who served as midwives to the nation of Israel. Called before Pharaoh, the most powerful person in Egypt, they were instructed to kill all the newborn Hebrew boys they helped to deliver. But their reverence for God was greater than their fear of Pharaoh and they determined not to obey his command. It was more important to them to please God than to earn the favor of an earthly ruler.

Are you allowing the fear of some person or situation to keep you from obeying the

Lord? Does the fear of your inadequacies inhibit you from serving God right where you are? Remember the promises of His Word: "I can do all things through Christ who strengthens me" (Philippians 4:13). "For God has not given us a spirit of fear, but of power and of love and of a sound mind" (2 Timothy 1:7). When you encounter a fearful situation, fill your mind with these promises. The God Who created and redeemed you is able to give you whatever it takes to overcome your fears and do what you know pleases Him.

Worldly danger may intimidate you, but godly fear can help you do what is right.

Reflections/Prayer Requests

_____

_____

_____

_____

_____

_____

_____

_____

_____

DAY 3

Exodus 1:20-21

Therefore God dealt well with the midwives, and the people multiplied and grew very mighty. And so it was, because the midwives feared God, that He provided households for them.

Reaping What You Sow

When a farmer sows corn, assuming he does what's necessary to cultivate the soil and the weather cooperates, he will reap a bountiful supply of corn in the fall. The same is true for milo, wheat, soybeans or any other crop. The laws of agriculture dictate that we reap what we sow.

The same is true in the spiritual world. We reap what we sow. Because of their reverence for God, the Hebrew midwives sowed compassion and mercy. In turn, God demonstrated the same toward them. He "established households for them" (NASB). In a patriarchal society like Israel, households were usually traced through the male lineage. But in return for their good deeds, God arranged for their descendants to trace their origins back to these two women.

Things haven't changed. Today we still reap what we sow, even in our earthly life. If we've abused our bodies with drugs or alcohol, it eventually catches up with us. On the other hand if we've sown good things such as kindness, we will receive good things back.

But there is also an ultimate time of reaping. For the Christian it will be at the Judgment Seat of Christ (2 Corinthians 5:10). For the non-Christian it will be at the Great White Throne Judgment (Revelation 20:11-15). In both situations God's judgment will be based on the things we have done. Works are not the basis for our salvation, but they are the basis for our rewards, or the loss of rewards.

So be like the Hebrew midwives. Show kindness to others just for the sake of kindness, and because of your love for God. He won't forget it.

If you want a good crop, you must sow good seed.

Reflections/Prayer Requests

_____

_____

_____

_____

_____

_____

_____

DAY 4

The Salvation Boat

Boats have played an important role in God's plan of salvation through the centuries. Genesis 6 tells of Noah's enormous ark (450 feet long, 45 feet high and 75 feet wide), which God used to save eight members of the human race during the flood that overwhelmed the world.

Exodus 2 describes a much smaller boat—actually no more than a reed basket covered with pitch to make it waterproof. But it played an important role in saving the life of baby Moses, whom God used as an adult to bind together a ragtag group of people into the nation of Israel. And out of this nation came Jesus, the Messiah and Savior.

Jesus Himself is also compared with a boat. In his first epistle, Peter reminds his readers of the ark that saved eight people from the flood. Then he says, "There is also an antitype which now saves us, namely baptism (not the removal of the filth of the flesh [i.e., not the literal physical baptism] but the answer of a good conscience toward God), through the resurrection of Jesus Christ" (1 Peter 3:21).

We are baptized (literally "put" or "placed") into Christ at the time of our salvation. He becomes our boat. Just as the ark saved Noah and his family from the wrath of the flood and the basket-boat saved Moses from certain death in the Nile, so Christ offers us a place of safety from the wrath that God will someday pour out on sin (Romans 5:9-10; Revelation 6:17).

The question you need to ask yourself is, "Am I in the boat or am I in the water?" Have you received Christ as your Savior? Will you be saved from God's wrath to come because you are safely "in Christ Jesus"? Only Jesus can keep you afloat when troubled waters come. Trust Him as your Savior and begin to enjoy new life in God's ark of salvation.

When the water threatens to overwhelm you, the only safe place is in the boat.

Reflections/Prayer Requests

_____

_____

_____

_____

_____

DAY 5

Exodus 2:5-6

Then the daughter of Pharaoh came down to wash herself at the river. And her maidens walked along the river's side; and when she saw the ark among the reeds, she sent her maid to get it. And when she had opened it, she saw the child, and behold, the baby wept. So she had compassion on him, and said, "This is one of the Hebrews' children."

Pity Power

A fictitious story is told of a man who fell into a pit and couldn't get himself out. A subjective person came along and said, "I feel for you, down there." An objective person came by and said, "It's logical that someone would fall down there." A mathematician passed by and stopped long enough to calculate how the man fell into the pit. A news reporter visited and wanted the exclusive story on his pit. A scientist heard about the situation and calculated the pressure necessary (pounds per square inch) to get the man out of the pit. A geologist advised him to appreciate the rock strata in the pit. An evasive person came along but avoided the subject of the pit altogether. A self-pitying person informed the man, "You haven't seen anything until you've seen my pit!" Then Jesus came by, saw the man in the pit and lifted him out.

Compassion must be yoked to action. Pharaoh's daughter, even though a pagan, coupled her compassion for a condemned Hebrew child with action. She drew him out of the water and raised him as her own son. She understood what it meant to put feet to her feeling.

Jesus always followed His compassion with action. The gospels tell us eight times that Jesus "had compassion," and each time He responded by healing the sick, feeding the hungry or providing wisdom for their spiritual ignorance.

When you look around and see those in need, don't stop with simply feeling pity—do something. Take a meal to someone just out of the hospital. Visit an elderly person who can no longer get out and about. Join those who protest abortion. Educate yourself and vote for those who reflect your values.

Today, ask God to touch your heart with a need—and then do something about it!

Don't just feel something, do something.

Reflections/Prayer Requests

_____

_____

_____

_____

DAY 6

Exodus 2:8-9

*And Pharaoh's daughter said to her, "Go."
So the maiden went and called the child's
mother. Then Pharaoh's daughter said to her,
"Take this child away and nurse him for me,
and I will give you your wages." So the
woman took the child and nursed him.*

The Omni God

Theologians use three words that begin
with the prefix "omni," all based on Scripture,
to describe God. "Omnipotent" declares that
He is all powerful. No one nor anything is
stronger than God. Through the prophet
Jeremiah, God said, "Behold, I am the Lord,
the God of all flesh. Is there anything too hard
for Me?" (Jeremiah 32:27). The implied
answer is no!

God is also described as "omnipresent"
(present everywhere). The psalmist asks,
"Where can I go from Your Spirit? Or where
can I flee from Your presence?" (Psalm 139:7).
He goes on to say, "If I ascend into heaven,
You are there; if I make my bed in hell,
behold, You are there. If I take the wings of
the morning, and dwell in the uttermost parts
of the sea, even there Your hand shall lead
me, and Your right hand shall hold me" (vv. 8-
10). No perilous pit is so deep or mountain
peak so high that God is not there.

Furthermore, God is "omniscient" (all-knowing). Embedded in this descriptive term is the root word *science,* which means knowledge. There is nothing that God doesn't know. Jeremiah confesses, "Who would not fear You, O King of the nations? For this is Your rightful due. For among all the wise men of the nations, and in all their kingdoms, there is none like You" (Jeremiah 10:7).

It is in this "omni" God that Jochebed, the mother of Moses, placed her trust; and He not only returned her son to her, but arranged circumstances so that she got paid to care for her own child. Only the God of all gods could do that.

No challenge is too great for an omnipotent, omniscient, omnipresent God. If you are faced today with a difficult problem, place it in God's hands and let the omni God work out the solution. You can be sure that no detail will be overlooked or loose end left untied. God's answers are always far more satisfying than anything we might be able to accomplish.

The power behind you is greater than the challenge ahead of you.

Reflections/Prayer Requests

_____

_____

_____

15

DAY 7

Exodus 2:11-12

Now it came to pass in those days, when Moses was grown, that he went out to his brethren and looked at their burdens. And he saw an Egyptian beating a Hebrew, one of his brethren. So he looked this way and that way, and when he saw no one, he killed the Egyptian and hid him in the sand.

Hiding Sin

A group of adults was asked, "Would you cheat on your income taxes if you knew for sure you would not be caught?" The majority said yes. It would seem that the prevailing philosophy is, "It's OK to do wrong if don't get caught."

Moses apparently agreed. He first looked "this way and that way" to make sure there were no witnesses; then he slew an Egyptian who was abusing a Hebrew slave. In addition, Moses hid the body in the sand, hoping to conceal his crime. Without proof of the crime, he seemed to reason, there was no crime.

There is one problem with this line of reasoning—it leaves out God. He has placed within us a small voice called "conscience." We may ignore that voice; we may keep so busy we think we can't hear it, but in the process we use up so much emotional energy that we damage our bodies. Doctors agree that up to 75 percent of their patients with chronic illnesses have no biological basis for their complaints. Instead, feelings of guilt and regret are at the root of their problems.

God's plan is for us to confess our sins, not hide them. Confession results not only in forgiveness but also cleansing. We don't have to carry a load of guilt around because it's washed away in the blood of Christ.

If you have a hidden sin, confess it to God. He is always willing to forgive sin when you truly repent and to wipe away the guilt that accompanies it (1 John 1:9). Confession will do wonders for your body as well as your spirit.

You don't have to put up with the smell of your sins if you come clean before God.

Reflections/Prayer Requests

_____

_____

_____

_____

_____

_____

DAY 8

Your Sins Will Find You Out

Greek mythology maintains that a young Spartan boy on his way to school found an orphaned lion cub. Hiding it under his toga, he slipped into the classroom and busied himself with his lessons. Part way through the morning the boy fell over dead. His teacher discovered that the lion cub had eaten into the boy's side even though the student refused to acknowledge anything was wrong.

Moses also tried to hide his sin. He first killed an Egyptian and then hid his body in the sand. But within 24 hours he realized, "Surely this thing is known!"

No matter how carefully we try to hide it, sin has a way of coming to the surface. It's like a drug smuggler who was trying to outrun the Coast Guard. When he saw he would probably be caught, he began throwing the bales of cotton that contained the illegal drugs overboard. Instead of sinking, however, the bales floated—forming a line of evidence that led directly to his boat.

Rather than hiding our sin, God would have us confess it and turn from it. Is there a secret sin in your life that is gnawing away at your heart? Confess it to God and ask His forgiveness. It would also be wise to confess it to a trusted friend, pastor or counselor who could hold you accountable for turning away from it.

God can forgive any sin except the one you refuse to acknowledge.

Reflections/Prayer Requests

_____

_____

_____

_____

_____

_____

_____

_____

_____

DAY 9

Exodus 2:15

When Pharaoh heard of this matter, he sought to kill Moses. But Moses fled from the face of Pharaoh and dwelt in the land of Midian.

Losing the Good Life

The state of Nebraska proudly proclaims that its residents enjoy "the good life." In 1995, however, the Nebraska Department of Correctional Services reported that 2,673 adults were shut away from this "good life" because of crimes they chose to commit. These people found, tragically, that sin can cause them to lose the good life that others enjoy.

Moses found the same truth. Rescued from death as an infant by Pharaoh's daughter, he was brought up with all the opportunities and privileges that wealth and rank could provide. For 40 years he lived the life of a prince, but in a fit of anger he killed a man—and lost it all. He became a fugitive from justice and an exile in the land of Midian. Banished from both the palace and his people, he was unable to help his Hebrew brothers for another 40 years.

When tempted by sin, we need to think about the good life we might lose. Sin can banish us from our home and loved ones. Choosing to do wrong can cost us our freedom and even our lives.

Most of all, sin will separate us from our fellowship with God. Ultimately, no life can truly be "good" unless it's lived out in the presence of God. An intimate relationship with the Father through His Son, Jesus, provides the peace, security and purposefulness that are necessary to experience "the good life." Without question, a good life must be a godly life. Losing this good life is a high price to pay for a short time of sin.

To enjoy the good life we must practice the godly life.

Reflections/Prayer Requests

_____

_____

_____

_____

_____

_____

_____

_____

_____

_____

DAY 10

Exodus 2:16-17
Now the priest of Midian had seven daughters.
And they came and drew water, and they filled
the troughs to water their father's flock. Then
the shepherds came and drove them away; but
Moses stood up and helped them, and
watered their flock.

And Justice for All

When we recite the pledge of allegiance, we firmly declare that we are committed to "liberty and justice for all." Yet our society does not practice what it proclaims. Pornography, for example, is a four billion dollar business in the United States, yet it degrades and exploits women and children—making them slaves to the perverted passions of a small but powerful group of individuals. Where is the justice in this? Abortions, which take the lives of helpless unborn children, are performed at the rate of more than 3,000 a day. Who can argue that these innocent ones are being treated justly?

Moses also encountered a situation of injustice. As he fled out into the Midian desert, he came across a well used to water the flocks of sheep that grazed in the area. This water was shared by numerous shepherds, among whom was a group of seven sisters, the daughters of a Midianite priest, Reuel. However, when these shepherdesses had gone to the hard work of drawing water up from the well and filling the troughs for their flocks, the other shepherds would drive them away and take it for themselves. Moses put a stop to this injustice and even replenished what had been taken from them.

God expects Christians to stand up for justice. In Isaiah 56:1 the Lord commands, "Keep justice, and do righteousness, for My salvation is about to come, and My righteousness to be revealed." The Book of Proverbs goes so far as to declare that those who sanction injustices are an "abomination to the Lord" (17:15).

While you cannot be personally involved in righting every injustice, ask God where and how He would have you expend your efforts. If you oppose abortion, for example, volunteer at a crisis pregnancy center. If you are burdened by the spread of pornography, initiate a petition to remove the pornographic magazines from your local store or gas station. While we each may have limited time and resources, we can all do something.

For injustice to triumph, good men need only to do nothing.

Reflections/Prayer Requests

_____

_____

_____

DAY 11

Exodus 2:21-22
Then Moses was content to live with the man,
and he gave Zipporah his daughter to Moses.
And she bore him a son, and he called his
name Gershom; for he said, "I have been a
stranger in a foreign land."

Just Passing Through

An American tourist in Israel was eager to meet a famous rabbi. Just days before the man was to return to the United States, a visit with the rabbi was arranged. When the day and hour arrived, the man was ushered into the apartment where the rabbi was staying. Looking around, the tourist was surprised by the lack of furnishings. As the meeting was about to close, the man could contain his curosity no longer. "Rabbi, if I might ask, where is your furniture?"

"Where is yours?" the rabbi shot back.

"Oh, I don't live here," the tourist replied. "I'm just passing through."

"So am I," the rabbi said.

Moses realized that the wilderness of Midian was not his home, nor was the land of Egypt. The writer of Hebrews says, "By faith Moses, when he became of age, refused to be called the son of Pharaoh's daughter, choosing rather to suffer affliction with the people of God than to enjoy the passing pleasures of sin, esteeming the reproach of Christ greater riches than the treasures in Egypt; for he looked to the reward" (11:24-26). Like Abraham, he looked forward to a heavenly country and a city whose builder and maker is God.

Where do you call home? If possessions are the criteria, many Christians are firmly entrenched here on earth. Jesus said, "For where your treasure is, there your heart will be also" (Matthew 6:21). An anonymous author, approaching the latter years of his life, wrote in great remorse: "How I've wasted my life. . . I have pursued shadows and entertained myself with dreams. I have been treasuring up dust and sporting myself with the wind. I might have grazed with the beasts of the fields, or sung with the birds of the woods, to much better purposes than any for which I have lived." I wonder how many Christians might say the same.

Perhaps God is asking you to simplify your life. Are there earthly treasures that you might turn into heavenly investments? You'll never regret that decision.

Earthly sacrifices pay heavenly dividends.

Reflections/Prayer Requests

DAY 12

Exodus 2:24-25

So God heard their groaning, and God remembered His covenant with Abraham, with Isaac, and with Jacob. And God looked upon the children of Israel, and God acknowledged them.

Precious Promises

March 11, 1942, was a dark and gloomy day on Corregidor. The Pacific theater of war was threatening and bleak. One island after another had been forced into submission. The enemy was now confidently marching into the Philippines. Surrender was inevitable. The commanding officer of the Allied forces, Gen. Douglas MacArthur, had only three words for his comrades as he stepped into the escape boat destined for Australia: "I shall return."

A little more than 2½ years later, on October 20, 1944, he stood once again on Philippine soil after landing safely at Leyte Island. This is what he said: "This is the voice of freedom, General MacArthur speaking. People of the Philippines, I have returned!" MacArthur kept his word. Regardless of the odds against him, he was determined to make good on his promise.

If mortal men with all their limitations can keep their promises, how much more so can the God of Abraham, Isaac, Jacob and Moses. God had committed Himself to the people of Israel; He had promised to bring them out of the land of Egypt (Genesis 46:4), and He would not fail.

There are more than 7,000 promises in the Bible. Some of these are made explicitly to individuals; others are made to nations such as Israel. Most of them, however, can be claimed by all believers—promises such as "Lo, I am with you always, even to the end of the age" (Matthew 28:20); " My God shall supply all your need according to His riches in glory by Christ Jesus" (Philippians 4:19); " The peace of God, which surpasses all understanding, will guard your hearts and minds through Christ Jesus" (Philippians 4:7).

As you read through your Bible, underline each promise as you come across it. Each day pick a promise to meditate upon, and at the end of the day take a few moments to thank God for being faithful to that promise. God is the greatest promise keeper of all.

God makes a promise: faith believes it, hope anticipates it, patience quietly awaits it.

Reflections/Prayer Requests

_____

_____

_____

DAY 13

Exodus 3:1

Now Moses kept the flock of Jethro his father-in-law, the priest of Midian. And he led the flock to the back of the desert, and came to Horeb, the mountain of God.

Bloom Where You Are

The great reformer John Knox never entered a pulpit until he was 40 years old. Some biographers maintain that during this time of obscurity, God was kindling the flame in his heart that would set on fire all of Scotland. After he began his public ministry, Knox was instrumental in leading the Kirk (Church) of Scotland into the Protestant faith and founded what became known as Presbyterianism.

Moses had a similar experience. Before God used him publicly, Moses spent 40 years caring for his father-in-law's sheep. Was he wasting his time? Not in the least. During the years he tended these obstinate animals on the back side of the desert he was learning patience and wisdom. He would need these traits later to lead an equally stiff-necked group of Jewish refugees out of Egypt and to the borders of the Promised Land.

If God has placed you in obscure circumstances, take heart. Do all you can where you are. There is no place so buried that it doesn't need a witness for Christ. No one is so far from God that he or she cannot benefit from your persistent prayers. You can be assured that the lessons you learn and the disciplines you develop in the obscure places of life will prepare you for greater things ahead. Bloom where you are and someday God will make you a bouquet.

If you don't serve God where you are, you probably won't serve Him someplace else.

Reflections/Prayer Requests

_____

_____

_____

_____

_____

_____

_____

_____

_____

_____

_____

DAY 14

Exodus 3:2-3

And the Angel of the Lord appeared to him in a flame of fire from the midst of a bush. So he looked, and behold, the bush burned with fire, but the bush was not consumed. Then Moses said, "I will now turn aside and see this great sight, why the bush does not burn."

Nothing Hidden

Hide-and-seek is fun for children. When we were young my brother and I especially enjoyed playing this game on a warm summer's evening. The gathering darkness helped hide our efforts to steal back to home base, where we would be "ole-ole-in-free."

But God doesn't play games, especially hide-and-seek. Throughout human history God has been revealing Himself rather than hiding Himself. When He appeared to Moses, it was not in some subtle mystical fashion; it was in a burning bush that Moses couldn't have missed.

George Macdonald wrote, "God hides nothing. His very work from the beginning is revelation—a casting aside of veil after veil, a showing to men of truth after truth. On and on from fact divine He advances, until at length in His Son, Jesus, He unveils His very face."

God wants to reveal Himself to you as well. If He seems to be veiled or hidden, first check to see if you know His Son, Jesus, as your personal Savior. It is only through Him that we have the privilege of drawing near to the Father (John 14:6). Then search your heart to see if some unconfessed sins may be dimming your view. Like winter frost on a window, sin keeps us from seeing clearly the Person of God. Finally, spend quality time in His Word. Nothing reveals God more completely than the Bible.

Only those who do not want to see God cannot see God.

Reflections/Prayer Requests

_____

_____

_____

_____

_____

_____

_____

_____

_____

_____

_____

DAY 15

Exodus 3:4

So when the Lord saw that he turned aside to look, God called to him from the midst of the bush and said, "Moses, Moses!" And he said, "Here I am."

Double Delight

I have a confession to make. I'm a chocoholic. I've never met a piece of chocolate I didn't like. The only thing more enticing than chocolate are those things that claim to be "double chocolate." This presents alluring options such as Double Dark Chocolate, Double Chocolate Swirl or my favorite, Double Dutch Chocolate. It just goes to prove that some things are so good that you can improve on them only by doubling what you already have.

God's call on our lives is also one of those things. As Moses approached to investigate the burning bush that was not consumed (Exodus 3:2-3), God called out to him, "Moses, Moses!" A double call. Moses was left with no doubt in his mind about whom God wanted—it was him!

God also has a double call on our lives. He calls us first to salvation. The apostle Paul said, "whom He called, these He also justified" (Romans 8:30). What a delight to know that our salvation does not rest on our frail efforts but on God's effective call.

Then He also calls us to service. Ephesians 2:10 declares, "For we are His workmanship, created in Christ Jesus for good works, which God prepared beforehand that we should walk in them." How marvelous to know that God has a plan for every Christian, including you. You need not wonder if you have a reason for living; God has it all laid out. There is no greater joy than walking in God's plan for your life.

Don't settle just for salvation; God saved you for service.

Refections/Prayer Requests

_____

_____

_____

_____

_____

_____

_____

_____

_____

_____

DAY 16

Exodus 3:5-6

Then He said, "Do not draw near this place. Take your sandals off your feet, for the place where you stand is holy ground." Moreover He said, "I am the God of your father—the God of Abraham, the God of Isaac, and the God of Jacob." And Moses hid his face, for he was afraid to look upon God.

Holy Ground

When worshipers or visitors come to many religious shrines in the Middle East, it is required of them to remove their shoes and leave them outside. The dirt and grime that accumulate on the soles of their shoes are not allowed inside a holy site. People there show their reverence and awe by removing anything impure before coming into the presence of the one they worship.

That is why God told Moses, "Take off your shoes, for this is holy ground." Wherever God is, whether in a burning bush or a stained glass cathedral, it is holy ground. It is a place of wonder and even terror, unsuited for anything polluted or dirty.

When we come into God's presence to worship, we, too, are treading on holy ground. In Western culture we would not likely remove our shoes, but we do need to

34

clean our minds. Pollutants from television, magazines and elsewhere quickly build up a film of dirt. If left unchecked, they produce a layer of dirty residue that defiles our hearts and minds. The filth of this world has no place in the presence of a pure and holy God.

Our visits to God's house are a good reminder to clean out any dirt that may have accumulated in our lives. Rather than drag these defilers onto holy ground, we need to confess them and be cleansed. Let's treat any place we encounter the awesome God as holy ground and act accordingly.

A cleansed mind is the most appropriate thing you can wear to church.

Reflections/Prayer Requests

_____

_____

_____

_____

_____

_____

_____

_____

DAY 17

Exodus 3:7

And the Lord said: "I have surely seen the oppression of My people who are in Egypt, and have heard their cry because of their taskmasters, for I know their sorrows."

Acquainted With Grief

A very angry man came to his pastor and demanded to know, "Where was God when my son was killed?" Knowing the hurt and sorrow behind that question, the pastor gently replied, "The same place that He was when His Son died."

There is nothing that you or I can experience that God has not already experienced through His Son. Speaking of His people, God told Moses, "For I know their sorrows." This is much more than an intellectual knowledge; it is a personal knowledge. It is not the knowledge gleaned by an objective bystander, but from feeling the pain of every cruel blow, the frustration of every unjust decision and the fear of every helpless slave before his master. God bore with His people their every sorrow.

Are you grieving today over a personal betrayal? Jesus understands—He was betrayed by one in His innermost circle. Are you hurt by an unjust decision? Jesus can identify with that—He was totally innocent yet condemned to die a criminal's death. Are you grieving the loss of a close friend? Jesus wept at the death of His friend Lazarus. Are you suffering from a feeling of loneliness? Jesus knows what you're going through because He was separated from His Father by sin on the cross. He cried out, "My God, My God, why have you forsaken me?" (Matthew 27:46).

Turn your sorrows over to the One who understands them best. He will not brush them aside lightly because He has felt the pain they cause. But the One who is acquainted with all our griefs is also the One who can heal them. Find in Him the comfort to survive the hurt and the power to become a whole person again.

Christ can do wonders with your broken heart if you give Him all the pieces.

Reflections/Prayer Requests

_____

_____

_____

_____

_____

_____

_____

DAY 18

Exodus 3:8-9

*"So I have come down to deliver them out of
the hand of the Egyptians, and to bring them
up from that land to a good and large land, to
a land flowing with milk and honey, to the
place of the Canaanites and the Hittites and
the Amorites and the Perizzites and the Hivites
and the Jebusites. Now therefore, behold, the
cry of the children of Israel has come to Me,
and I have also seen the oppression with which
the Egyptians oppress them."*

Someone's Watching Over Me

Cheryl Cassiday is a registered nurse in
Chadron, Nebraska. One cold February
afternoon she arrived at the Chadron Arts
Center to pick up her daughter, Rachael,
from her dance lessons. "I had another
errand to run," she said, "but as I turned the
corner I chose not to pick up the milk." That
decision probably saved the lives of her
daughter and eight other people. Instead of
waiting in the car as she usually did, Cheryl
went into the dance studio. There she
found her daughter, six other students, the
dance instructor and the instructor's father
all overcome by carbon monoxide poisoning. With help from the family across the
street, she was able to pull everyone out of
the building and revive them. Mrs.

38

Cassiday's conclusion: "Somebody was watching out for these girls besides me."

Moses discovered the same thing. Somebody was watching over the people of Israel. God told him, "I have seen the oppression with which the Egyptians oppress them."

The God who created human sight is not blind. In fact, nothing escapes His eyes. The psalmist says, "His eyes observe the nations" (Psalm 66:7), and the writer of Chronicles notes, "For the eyes of the Lord run to and fro throughout the whole earth, to show Himself strong on behalf of those whose heart is loyal to Him" (2 Chronicles 16:9). Not for a moment are God's people out of His sight!

If you have fears and worries, remember Somebody is watching over you. Your Heavenly Father will never forget you nor forsake you. At the appropriate time and in His own way, He will deliver you from all your troubles.

While you are in the fire, God's eye is on the thermostat.

Reflections/Prayer Requests

_____

_____

_____

DAY 19

Exodus 3:11

But Moses said to God, "Who am I that I should go to Pharaoh, and that I should bring the children of Israel out of Egypt?"

Just a Nobody

On several occasions I have visited Mt. Rushmore in the Black Hills of South Dakota. Each time I looked up into those massive faces of George Washington, Thomas Jefferson, Theodore Roosevelt and Abraham Lincoln, I felt very small and incredibly insignificant.

Moses must have felt the same way as the enormousness of what God was asking him to do sank in. The original handful of people who had gone down to Egypt in the days of Joseph had grown to more than 600,000 men, plus women and children. Add to that the "mixed multitude" that would join them, and some scholars estimate that more than a million people made that historic exodus out of Egypt.

Moses knew that even if Pharaoh finally let these people go, the responsibility of organizing, transporting and providing food and water for them and their livestock would be staggering. No wonder Moses said, "Who am I, Lord?" Today he might have said, "Lord, I'm just a nobody. I don't have the skills. I can't do what You want me to do."

Isn't that typical? When God called Gideon, he replied, "O my Lord, how can I save Israel? Indeed my clan is the weakest in Manasseh, and I am the least in my father's house" (Judges 6:15). When God called Jeremiah, the prophet-to-be said, "Ah, Lord God! Behold, I cannot speak, for I am a youth" (Jeremiah 1:6).

It's not unusual to feel inadequate for the tasks God gives us. It's meant to be that way! God wants us to learn that we can do anything, but only as long as we let Him do it through us. Open yourself to God and let Him open the possibilities to you.

God can do more with a "nobody" than anyone else can do with a "somebody."

Reflections/Prayer Requests

_____

_____

_____

_____

_____

_____

_____

DAY 20

Exodus 3:12a

So He said, "I will certainly be with you. . . ."

Never Alone

Moses was afraid. Having lived in the palace of Pharaoh for 40 years, he knew well the results of raising the wrath of such a powerful man. Furthermore, he knew that his request to let God's people go would not be a popular one. God's solution for this fear and trepidation: His own presence. He assured Moses, "I will certainly be with you."

Believers through the centuries have found God's presence to be the source of courage and strength in the midst of otherwise insurmountable challenges. When David Livingstone returned from Africa, a student at Glasgow University asked him, "What sustained you during those years in Africa?" Livingstone replied, "Shall I tell you what sustained me amidst the toil and hardship and loneliness of my life? It was the promise, 'Lo, I am with you always, even unto the end of the ages.'"

Life can be very difficult. Fears press in from every side. Discouragement grabs us by the soul and drags us down. But still God is with us. His presence is assured. Henry van Dyke noted, "Happy and strong and brave shall we be—able to endure all things, and to do all things—if we believe that every day, every hour, every moment of our life is in God's hands."

If you are going through dark times today, know that God is with you. His grace will meet all your needs, and His strength will be sufficient for your every trial. There is never a moment when you are out of His sight or out of His thoughts.

When you reach the end of yourself you will find it's only the beginning of God.

Reflections/Prayer Requests

_____

_____

_____

_____

_____

_____

_____

_____

_____

_____

_____

DAY 21

Exodus 3:12b

*". . . And this shall be a sign to you that
I have sent you: When you have brought
the people out of Egypt, you shall serve
God on this mountain."*

Where Am I?

I do a lot of traveling both overseas and in the United States. Sometimes the trips get very lengthy and involved with multiple airplane connections and layovers. Thus it is reassuring to look at my travel itenerary and discover that I'm still on track. I may not have arrived yet but I can tell I'm headed in the right direction.

Moses needed this kind of assurance as well. After all the struggles in Egypt, he needed to know he was still following God's itenerary. Therefore God instructed him to bring the people out of Egypt and return to Mt. Sinai where he saw the burning bush. When they got to the mountain they were to "serve" Him. This was God's proof that they were headed in the right direction and that He would lead them into the Promised Land.

Sometimes we too get discouraged in our spiritual journey and wonder if maybe we've lost God somehow. Could it be that we're only fooling ourselves in thinking that He has a personal interest in us? Satan would certainly like for us to think that way.

That's when we need to take a look at where we are spiritually. Are we further along than when we first began? Perhaps we aren't where we would like to be in our walk with the Lord, but the fact that we aren't where we used to be is proof that God is with us. The apostle Paul said in Philippians 1:6, "Being confident of this very thing, that He who has begun a good work in you will complete it until the day of Jesus Christ." Don't get discouraged that you haven't arrived, just make sure you're headed the right direction. God will take care of the rest; He always finishes what He starts.

It's not where you are but where you are going that counts.

Reflections/Prayer Requests

_____

_____

_____

_____

_____

_____

DAY 22

Exodus 3:13

Then Moses said to God, "Indeed, when I come to the children of Israel and say to them, 'The God of your fathers has sent me to you,' and they say to me, 'What is His name?' what shall I say to them?"

Name Above All Names

Names are often unique to a given culture or society. If you hear the name Hassan or Muhammad, you identify a particular culture immediately. If the name is José or Carlos, another culture comes to mind. Names used in one culture are frequently not used in another.

In addition, names come and go. According to one source, the most popular names in the United States for children in 1995 were Emily and Jacob. The year before they were Ashley and Tyler. But while other names may rise and fall in popularity, God's name stays the same.

In the Bible, names usually reflected a person's character. For example, Nabal meant "fool"—and he was one (1 Samuel 25:25). Barnabas meant "son of encouragement"—and he was noted for his acts of encouragement (Acts 4:36).

When Moses wanted to know God's name so he could tell it to the Israelites, he really wanted to know God's character. What kind of a God was this One who spoke from a burning bush? If they were going to place their lives into His hands, they needed to know, "Can God be trusted?"

The Israelites found indeed that God is wholly trustworthy. For 40 years He cared for them as they wandered in the wilderness. You, too, will find Him trustworthy. God is as good as His name. Place your life, your future, your fortunes into His hands; He will never fail you. His is the name above all names.

Many people have different names, but there is only One name you can always trust.

Reflections/Prayer Requests

_____

_____

_____

_____

_____

_____

_____

_____

DAY 23

Exodus 3:14
And God said to Moses, "I AM WHO I AM."
And He said, "Thus you shall say to the chil-
dren of Israel, 'I AM has sent me to you.'"

The Great I AM

People tend to identify themselves by what is important to them. If you were to talk to a man, he would probably identify himself both by his name and his job. He might say, "Hi, I'm Robert Smith. I teach high school math." A woman would more likely identify herself in terms of relationships. She might say, "Hi, I'm Ellen Smith, Robert's wife," or, "Hi, I'm Darlene Jones, Jill's friend."

But God does neither. When Moses needed a name to take to the Israelites in Egypt, God said, "Tell them 'I AM' has sent you." God identifies Himself not by what He does or by His relationships, but rather by who He is. The name I AM can be taken to mean "I AM whatever you need." If you are hungry, I AM the Bread of Life (John 6:35). If you are thirsty, I AM the living water (John 4:10-14). If you are in bondage, I AM the One who sets the captives free (Luke 4:18).

God is the eternal I AM. He is for you whatever you need today, just as He was for Moses. And He will be for you tomorrow whatever you need then. Do you have a pressing need in your life? Whatever it is, be assured God can meet it. You may need peace during a troubled time (John 14:1, 27). You may need comfort in the midst of sorrow (Psalm 147:3). You may need to feel that someone loves you (John 15:13). God can meet all your needs; He is still the great I AM. Call upon Him and He will answer your need.

When you have the I AM, you have everything you need.

Reflections/Prayer Requests

_____

_____

_____

_____

_____

_____

_____

_____

_____

_____

_____

DAY 24

Exodus 3:18-20

"Then they will heed your voice; and you shall come, you and the elders of Israel, to the king of Egypt; and you shall say to him, 'The Lord God of the Hebrews has met with us; and now, please, let us go three days' journey into the wilderness, that we may sacrifice to the Lord our God.' But I am sure that the king of Egypt will not let you go, no, not even by a mighty hand. So I will stretch out My hand and strike Egypt with all My wonders which I will do in its midst; and after that he will let you go."

Get With the Program

"Get with the program" was a popular expression a few years ago. It meant that a person needed to understand what was going on around him and adjust his lifestyle or plans accordingly.

To fail to get with the program can be harmful, if not disastrous, to the person who is out of step. Pharaoh was a good example. God outlined His plans for Israel to Moses in verse 18. But God knew that Pharaoh would not cooperate. He would refuse to adjust his plans to fit God's program. Consequently, God said, "So I will stretch out My hand and strike Egypt with all My wonders which I will do in its midst; and after that he will let you go." It wasn't until the tragic death of the firstborn of Egypt that Pharaoh was willing to get with the program.

As Christians, you and I need to be in step with God's program. God has a plan for our lives, and only that plan will result in our greatest happiness. How can you discover His plan? By prayer, the counsel of godly friends and the guidance of His Word. Once we discover His plan we must then adjust our lifestyle accordingly. To reject God's program will bring only heartache and disappointment.

Are you actively seeking to follow God's program for your life? If so, that doesn't mean you will never experience setbacks or sorrow, but it does mean that when all is said and done, your life will have eternal significance. That makes it worth the effort to get with the program.

God provides the program; you provide the willingness.

Reflections/Prayer Requests

_____

_____

_____

_____

_____

_____

DAY 25

Exodus 4:1

Then Moses answered and said, "But suppose they will not believe me or listen to my voice; suppose they say, 'The Lord has not appeared to you.'"

What If

Have you ever found yourself playing the "what if" game? What if I have an accident? What if my check doesn't come? What if my child gets sick?

It's good to plan ahead. We all should have a contingency plan in most situations. But when God says, "Do this . . . ," there is no room for other contingencies. Options are not acceptable. God told Moses to deliver the Israelites from Egypt. But in response Moses began to say, "But suppose . . ."

"What ifs" often paralyze Christians. God calls them to teach a Sunday school class, but they begin to play "what if." "Suppose I can't keep control of the class." "Suppose I am not a good teacher." "Suppose an emergency comes up and I can't make it to class." Since any "what if" is a possibility— even the remote ones—they soon create "analysis paralysis." The possible disasters outweigh the potential good and we are left with an impossible situation. We freeze up and are unable or unwilling to make a decision.

Satan loves to get us so concerned about the "what ifs" that we are too afraid to follow God's will. However, if God has called us to a task, we can have the confidence that He will deal with the consequences as well. When Satan whispers in our ear, "What if?" how should we respond? How about, "So what? God will take care of it."

If God calls you, your "what ifs" are all taken care of.

Reflections/Prayer Requests

_____
_____
_____
_____
_____
_____
_____
_____
_____
_____
_____

DAY 26

Exodus 4:2

So the Lord said to him, "What is that in your hand?" And he said, "A rod."

Give What You've Got

When we think of giving to God, sometimes we fantasize about what we could do if only we had a lot of money. We're like the man who told his pastor, "I wish I could win a million dollars so I could give a tenth of it to the church." His pastor replied, "Why don't you just give a tenth of what you've got?" "Oh," the man said, "I need that to live on." Isn't that just like us? We're willing to give what we don't have, but God wants what we have.

When God confronted Moses on Mt. Sinai, Moses was just a poor shepherd. He had neither silver nor gold; he had no fine clothing; he had little to offer God—nothing but a rod that he used as a shepherd's staff. That was all he had, and that was all God asked for.

Yet with that simple rod God caused a hail storm that killed every unprotected person and animal in the land of Egypt (Exodus 9:23). With that simple staff God caused a plague of locusts that infested every field (10:13). And with Moses' rod God divided the Red Sea to permit the Israelites to cross on dry ground (14:16). Moses didn't have much to give, but when he gave it to God it became a lot.

If you don't have a great deal to give to God, don't hold back what you do have. God is not concerned about the size of your gift, just the size of your heart. Give to God what you have, and you will be blessed by what He does with it.

Little is much when God is in it.

Reflections/Prayer Requests

_____

_____

_____

_____

_____

_____

_____

_____

_____

_____

_____

_____

DAY 27

Exodus 4:3, 6, 9
*And He said, "Cast it on the ground." So he
cast it on the ground, and it became a serpent;
and Moses fled from it.*

*Furthermore the Lord said to him, "Now put
your hand in your bosom." And he put his
hand in his bosom, and when he took it out,
behold, his hand was leprous, like snow.*

*"And it shall be, if they do not believe even
these two signs, or listen to your voice, that
you shall take water from the river and pour
it on the dry land. And the water which
you take from the river will become blood
on the dry land."*

Beyond a Doubt

A little girl once defined faith as "believing in something you know isn't true."
Unfortunately, many people feel the same
way. In their opinion, the first step in
becoming a Christian is to turn off your
mind. But that's not what the Bible says.

Moses knew that he couldn't return to
Egypt after 40 years and expect the people
to accept what he was going to tell them.
He needed proof that he truly was bringing a message from God. Therefore, God
gave him three signs to show the people.
The first caused his staff to become a serpent; the second caused his hand to

become leprous; and the third changed water into blood.

God does not require anyone to make a leap into the unknown. That's foolishness, not faith. He never asks people to believe without evidence. Instead God says, "Come now, and let us reason together" (Isaiah 1:18). The word *reason* means to argue or to discuss in order to come to a sensible conclusion.

If you are struggling with doubt, look to the evidence. Creation proclaims the existence of God. The empty tomb assures us we have a risen Savior. Changed lives demonstrate God's love and mercy. The evidence is all around you. There is no reason to doubt. It only makes good sense to have faith in God.

Faith is believing in things unseen but not unprovable.

Reflections/Prayer Requests

_____

_____

_____

_____

_____

_____

Exodus 4:10

Then Moses said to the Lord, "O my Lord, I am not eloquent, neither before nor since You have spoken to Your servant; but I am slow of speech and slow of tongue."

Stuffed With a Lie

Someone has said, "An excuse is the skin of a truth stuffed with a lie." In other words, an excuse has all the outward appearance of truth, but inside it quickly loses that ring of authenticity. When you begin to probe beneath the surface—to explore the motives and purpose—it becomes obvious that the outer resemblance of an excuse is inconsistent with the inner reason.

Moses responded to God's call by posing a number of questions: Who shall I say sent me? What if they don't listen to me? How can I persuade them to believe me? These were legitimate concerns, of course, and they needed to be answered in order to get the job done.

But then Moses stooped to making excuses. In essence he said, "God, You can't use me. You need someone with greater abilities." On the surface this had the appearance of truth. Moses may really have had a speech impediment that made him difficult to understand, although that didn't appear to be the case when he stood before Pharaoh. But underneath this truth lay the real reason, the hidden reason— Moses simply didn't want to go. His wife and children were in Midian. Forty years had gone by and perhaps his interests in Egypt may have lessened. To top it off, he was 80 years old—not the time of life when you want to start such an undertaking. So he tried to excuse himself and angered God (Exodus 4:14).

As Moses learned, it's impossible to deceive God. He knows our thoughts and reads our motives. He sees through our excuses and exposes the true reasons for our actions or inactions. Ask God to search your heart and make your real reasons obvious to you. If you've been making excuses, it's time to ask His forgiveness and pray for strength to be obedient instead.

An excuse is no substitute for obedience.

Reflections/Prayer Requests

DAY 29

Exodus 4:11

So the Lord said to him, "Who has made man's mouth? Or who makes the mute, the deaf, the seeing, or the blind? Have not I, the Lord?"

Imperfect to Man, Perfect for God

Many famous people have had difficulties to overcome. Wilma Rudolph was one. A bout with polio as a child left her left leg crooked and her foot twisted inward, so she had to wear leg braces. It took seven years of painful therapy before she could walk without them. At age 12, Wilma tried out for a girls' basketball team but didn't make it. Determined to improve, she practiced with a girlfriend and two boys every day. The next year she made the team. When a college track coach saw her during a game, he talked her into letting him train her as a runner. By age 14 she had outrun the fastest sprinters in the United States. In 1956 Wilma made the U.S. Olympic team, but showed poorly. That bitter disappointment motivated her to work harder for the 1960 Olympics in Rome—and there Wilma Rudolph won three gold medals.

Moses also had a handicap to overcome. Some scholars suggest that perhaps he was a stutterer. In any event he felt his inability to speak effectively disqualified him from the task to which God called him. But God didn't agree. In effect He said to Moses, "Look, I made your mouth. If I had wanted you to be eloquent, I could have made you that way. Instead I chose you to serve Me just as you are."

Perhaps you are physically challenged in some way. You may have despaired of ever serving God. Rather than bemoaning your inability, recognize God's great ability. He can use you even with your limitations. In fact, He may turn your perceived handicap into a great blessing to others.

Give God what you have and ask Him to use your special circumstances to glorify Himself. God could have made your body perfect, and for His unique purposes for you, He did!

It's a willing heart, not a perfect body, that serves God best.

Reflections/Prayer Requests

_____

_____

_____

_____

_____

_____

DAY 30

Exodus 4:12
Now therefore, go and I will be with your mouth and teach you what you shall say:

An Ever Present Help

Walter Winchell defined a friend as "one who walks in when others walk out." But there are times when even proven friends can't help us. Sometimes we're far from our friends in a distant city and we need help. When we sit beside the deathbed of a loved one and our friends try to comfort us. often they can't actually help. No matter where we are or how difficult our experiences, however, God can help US.

Moses faced the overwhelming task of confronting Pharaoh and demanding the release of the Hebrew people. Everything was on the line: his leadership, his integrity. his life. as well as the future of the nation of Israel. Surely those who cared about him sympathized with the situation, but none could help. Only God could say, "I will be with your mouth and teach you what you shall say."

God's people always have found that when everything else is taken from them— all their loved ones and possessions are gone God still is "a very present help in trouble" (Ps. 46:1, cf. Heb. 4:16). In the biography of Corrie ten Boom, she describes her thoughts after the death of her sister Betsie in a concentration camp: "I was not afraid to die. The valley of the shadow of death had no terror for me. Jesus had carried me through these prisons. He would stay with me until the end, or better. the new heginning."

It's when you are at the end of yourself that you discover God is just beginning. Obey His will; He will provide the way. As the hymn writer reminds us, "Fear not. I am with thee—O be not dismayed for I am thy God, I will still give thee aid. I'll strengthen thee, help thee and cause thee to stand. Upheld by my gracious, omnipotent hand." That's quite a promise. Don't fail to claim it today.

When we have nothing left but God, we will find He is enough.

Reflections/Prayer Requests

_____

_____

_____

_____

_____

_____

DAY 31

Exodus 4:20

*Then Moses took his wife and his sons,
and set them upon an ass, and he returned to
the land of Egypt: and Moses took the rod
of God in his hand.*

From Ordinary to Extraordinary

A friend of mine in New York City is quite an artist. He keeps his eyes peeled on the streets of Manhattan for broken pieces of glass—pop bottles, smashed tail lights, even Vicks jars. He takes these worthless pieces of junk home, washes them and without reshaping them in any way, turns them into lovely stained glass mosaics of biblical scenes. Under his touch, the ordinary becomes extraordinary. What was of little value is now a thing of incredible beauty.

God does the same thing. His transforming power can take a shepherd's staff and make it the "rod of God." An ordinary shaft of wood becomes an extraordinary instrument to call forth plagues (Exodus 9:28), divide seas (14:16) and bring forth water from a rock (17:5-6).

The same is true for our lives. Under God's touch we become a "new creation" in

Christ (2 Corinthians 5:17)—not simply something made over or improved, but a totally new creature with supernatural abilities. When we receive Christ as our Savior, an extraordinary change begins to take place. No matter how ordinary we may consider our lives, God is able to create an extraordinary work of art out of us.

If you consider yourself ordinary, rejoice! You're just the kind of person God loves to use. He took ordinary fishermen and made them the pillars of the early Church. Today He empowers ordinary farmers, factory workers and housewives and makes them messengers of the Good News. With God, the ordinary is always extraordinary. Give thanks that you are an extraordinary person in Christ, and live above the ordinary.

God is the "extra" in the extraordinary.

Reflections/Prayer Requests

_____

_____

_____

_____

_____

_____

_____